THE KITCHEN
IDEA BOOK

THE KITCHEN
IDEA BOOK

Joanne Kellar Bouknight

The Taunton Press

To Neil

The Taunton Press
Inspiration for hands-on living™

Text © 2001 by Joanne Kellar Bouknight
Photos © 2001 by The Taunton Press, Inc., where noted
Illustrations © 2001 by The Taunton Press, Inc.

Printed in the United States of America
10 9 8 7 6 5 4

The Taunton Press, Inc., 63 South Main Street, PO Box 5506, Newtown, CT 06470-5506
e-mail: tp@taunton.com

The Kitchen Idea Book was originally published in hardcover
in 1999 by The Taunton Press, Inc.

Distributed by Publishers Group West

TITLE PAGE PHOTO
Reese Hamilton

DEDICATION PHOTO
Andrew McKinney

CONTENTS PHOTOS (left to right)
Markatos Photography, John Kane, Lizzie Himmel, Charles Miller,
Lizzie Himmel, Charles Miller, Charles Miller

INTRODUCTION PHOTOS
David Duncan Livingston (p. 2), Lizzie Himmel (p. 3), Derrill Bazzy
(p. 4, top), Roe A. Osborn (p. 4, bottom), Durston Saylor (p. 5)

COLOPHON PHOTO
Andrew McKinney

Library of Congress Cataloging-in Publication Data

Bouknight, Joanne Kellar.
        The kitchen idea book / Joanne Kellar Bouknight.
            p. cm.
        Includes bibliographical references.
        ISBN 1-56158-161-5 hardcover
        ISBN 1-56158-574-2 paperback
        1. Kitchens. I. Title.
TX653.B68   1999
643'.3—dc21   98-41873
                                                CIP

ACKNOWLEDGMENTS

Hundreds of people had a hand in the making of each of the hundreds of kitchens in this book, and I wish I could list them all. I appreciate their work, and I thank all who designed, built, fit up, and own these kitchens. Kitchen designers and photographers *are* listed in the back of this book. If I missed any of you, I apologize.

While many people contributed directly to this book, I'm especially grateful to the following, who were more than generous when I asked for contributions by way of advice, leads, photos, and details:

John Abrams of South Mountain Builders, Chilmark, Mass.; Austin Patterson Disston Architects, Southport, Conn.; Lou Ann Bauer, ASID, San Francisco, Calif.; Peter Bentel, Carol Rusche Bentel, and Paul Bentel of Bentel & Bentel Architects, Locust Valley, N.Y.; Alan Bouknight of Azzarone Contracting Corp., Mineola, N.Y; Lynn Bronfman of Today's Kitchens, Stamford, Conn.; Norma DeCamp Burns,

FAIA, Raleigh, N.C.; Peter Cardamone of Bluebell Kitchens, Springhouse, Pa.; Fu-Tung Cheng and Margaret Burnett of Cheng Design, Berkeley, Calif.; Peter Craz of Craz Woodworking, Holbrook, N.Y.; Dail Dixon, FAIA, of Dixon Weinstein Architects, Chapel Hill, N.C.; The Kennebec Co., Bath, Maine; John Leontiou of Form Ltd., Greenwich, Conn.; Debbie Lipner of Deborah T. Lipner, Ltd., Greenwich, Conn.; David Duncan Livingston, Mill Valley, Calif.; Louis Mackall of Breakfast Woodworks, Guilford, Conn.; Joeb Moore, Laura Kaehler, Neil Bouknight, George Dumitru, Lisa Mockler, and Michael Shuman of Kaehler/Moore Architects, Greenwich, Conn.; Liz and Rick O'Leary, Croton Falls, N.Y.; Lisa Oswald, Greenwich, Conn.; Laurel Quint of Q Design, Denver, Colo.; Buddy Rhodes and Susan Anderson of Buddy Rhodes Studio, Inc., San Francisco, Calif.; Durston Saylor, New York, N.Y.; Regina Schrambling, New York, N.Y.; Wendy Silver, Cos Cob Library, Cos Cob, Conn.; Paul Tesar,

Raleigh, N.C.; Rob Thallon, Eugene, Oreg.; and Defne Veral of Defne Veral Interiors, New Haven, Conn.

For the opportunity to write *The Kitchen Idea Book*, I thank the dedicated folks at The Taunton Press: namely, John Lively for the *Fine Homebuilding* hire and for sage writing advice; Jon Miller and Julie Trelstad for the initial proposal; Jim Childs and Carolyn Mandarano for separating the idea from the chaff; Steve Culpepper and Carol Kasper for an abundance of patience, persistence, and guidance; Peter Chapman for his good ear and dogged pursuit of accuracy; and Tom McKenna for editorial finesse. And thanks to Henry Roth for his unruffled existentialism and his thoughtful and beautiful design, which for me really nails down the concept of this book.

Many of the photos in this book come from the gold mine shot by Taunton's *Fine Homebuilding* staff. For photos and amplification, I thank all current and former editors of the

magazine, especially the folks I worked with during my *Fine Homebuilding* tenure: editor Kevin Ireton, the prolific Charles Miller, contributing editor Bruce Greenlaw, and art director Chuck Lockhart. Thanks also to editorial secretary Joyce McWilliam for her patience and legal pads.

For watercolor counsel, thanks to artist Lizzy Rockwell.

For their gifts of ideas, time, and patience, I can't even begin to give enough thanks to my friends and to my family, both near and far.

And for keeping me in kitchens, whether downstairs or at my desk, my deepest thanks and love to our school-age boys Neilie and Sebastian and, especially, to my husband Neil. He has been an untiring source of architectural insight and feedback, and he always gave me the time and encouragement I needed to work on this book. This is the year for our new kitchen.

CONTENTS

INTRODUCTION

These days, everyone seems to live in the kitchen. It's where we talk about things both trivial and important. It's where all parties end up. It's where the children want to be from the time they can bang on pots and pans until they're home from college. It's where the computer is, and it's where the mail gets sorted. Oh, and did I say, it's where meals are made and eaten?

The average kitchen design lasts 15 years. That means your kitchen is probably ready for an update. If you're like me, you spend hours in a kitchen that doesn't quite work. And you'd love to change that. You'd like to add eating space in the kitchen or reposition the appliances to eliminate gridlock around the refrigerator. Whatever the change you're considering, or if you're starting from the ground up with a new kitchen, you know that you have a hundred decisions to make.

This book isn't a coffee-table book, it's a kitchen-table book—a "cookbook" of kitchen details. Like kitchen-table wisdom, these kitchens are a combination of down-to-earth basics and sky's-the-limit ideas; I hope they will confirm your own ideas, help you when you've run out of ideas, or maybe even change your mind.

You'll find hundreds—thousands—of ideas to help you make decisions about layout, materials, and details. You'll understand style, see how kitchens work, and learn what makes a good-quality cabinet. You'll find ideas on how to trim the top of a cabinet or finish the edge of a countertop. You'll find new ways of incorporating appliances and adding light to dull kitchens.

What you won't find is some Platonic ideal of the efficient kitchen. Some people hate peninsulas, others love them. The kitchen triangle can be a boon or a bust for your situation. Determine your ideal, then compromise. Your kitchen may offer something more compelling than the perfect prep-cook-cleanup layout, such as a breathtaking view, a beautiful piece of kitchen equipment, a gigantic kitchen table, a budget, or existing space. As long as you're not cranking out meals for money, you can probably live with a little glitch in the plan. In our small kitchen, we have to swing out around the end of a long, skinny kitchen table each time we move between sink and stove, but we'll never get rid of that wonderful, wobbly table just to make a beeline between appliances (the exercise doesn't hurt, either).

Likewise, you probably know deep down that the latest in kitchen appliances and finishes is not a burning necessity for a kitchen that people love to be in. I remember an off-campus kitchen with an 18-in.-wide range, two running feet of countertop, and a bare bulb screwed into a ceiling fixture. But what meals! A pot-luck Thanksgiving dinner with a turkey whose posterior hung out of the tiny oven, the bread toasted over a gas flame during a tornado blackout and served with the first Beluga caviar any of us had tasted. Ambience is made by people and food, not by a granite island the size of Texas or a cold-water faucet by the cooktop.

On the other hand, anyone with a faucet by the cooktop loves it for filling pasta pots. And owners of big granite islands rejoice that they can prepare a flotilla of cookie sheets at the same time. The stove, always a status symbol, is again a compelling behemoth, a stainless-steel version of the black, cast-iron, coal-burning beauties of a century ago. Who hasn't justified the expense of something in the kitchen because it looks great and promises to perform better and faster?

Take a look at these kitchens for the critical pieces that make a kitchen belong to its owner. There's the restored enamel cast-iron sink with the two huge bowls and integral backsplash, the beautiful concrete half-wall that's speckled with bits of glass and air pockets, and the slender, oak Arts and Crafts kitchen table. While some of these kitchens took a big chunk of money to build, others were built on a shoestring budget. Whatever the cost, there's a cabinet, an appliance, a floor, a light fixture, or a layout that can inspire someone who's in the market for a new kitchen.

While some of these kitchens have been styled for picture-taking, most have not—beyond the basic spit-and-polish required when company's coming. These kitchens are all real, not "dream kitchens" put together for a designer showcase or a product ad.

As you look through this book, keep an eye on the three types of text. The main text provides basic information; sidebar text—boxed and shaded—provides excursions into particular aspects of the kitchen, from dumbwaiters to sink materials. For the nitty-gritty details in each photo, read the captions. That's where you'll find references to materials and design ideas that you may want to apply to your own kitchen. To find the designer of any kitchen shown here, check the credits in the back of the book.

Turn to *For More Information* on pp. 196-197 to find sources for both kitchen-design and kitchen-construction books and articles that can help in designing your kitchen. You'll also find a list of kitchen-related associations and a look at what I've found on the ever-expanding Web with regard to kitchens.

Even beyond these sources, keep looking at kitchens for ideas. Look in seasonal kitchen magazines, go to kitchen showrooms, take kitchen tours. Invite yourself over to look at kitchens. Sneak a peak under the sink and inside the refrigerator. Observe how handwashed dishes are drained and where garbage and recyclables are stored. Don't ignore older kitchens; some good ideas show up in the most unassuming places. My grandmother Ruby was quite short in later years, and her most trusted piece of kitchen equipment was a library stool, which scoots around freely but won't budge when you sit or stand on it. She set her garbage pail on the stool and pulled it around the kitchen to catch vegetable trimmings, coffee grounds, and spent paper towels. When she needed something in a wall cabinet, she'd remove the garbage pail and stand on the stool. Not only is mobile garbage a good idea, but a library stool is a safer means of acquiring height than a chair or folding stool.

Finally, when you do build your new kitchen, please don't take the tack that the town officials are out to get you. Building codes are meant for your safety—and for future occupants of your kitchen. There's a big plus side to developing a good, above-board, honest, talking relationship with the town planners, engineers, and inspectors. You'll not only learn something about local building practices and how your town works, but you may also find that Town Hall is agreeable to squeezing in your request for a variance before the Board of Adjustment takes off for the summer.

GREAT KITCHEN DESIGNS

Why a new kitchen? For starters, how about the lure of new, state-of-the-art appliances, cabinets, and countertop materials? Creating a completely new look is ample reason to rip out the old and one of the big thrills of owning a home. But even more important than a new six-burner cooktop or the latest solid-surface countertop is *space*. People want bigger kitchens these days. Big enough for two cooks, for children and homework, big enough for eating, paying bills, and just sitting around. Even if a new kitchen is just big enough for the basics, those basics no doubt include eating, playing, and working. That's what modern kitchens are for.

In this chapter I'll cover the basics of designing that new kitchen, big or small. First, we'll set the style. Does a contemporary kitchen suit the house? Is Shaker style more fitting? Or is a mix of new and traditional the best solution? Next, we'll lay out the kitchen. Then we'll consider how the kitchen connects with the rest of the house. There is a growing nostalgia for the Colonial *keeping* room: a room for work, play, and cooking, complete with fireplace. On the other hand, a separate kitchen makes it easier to conceal dirty cookware during a dinner party. Finally, think fresh air and sunlight. No matter how it fits in the house, it's a rare kitchen that doesn't benefit from a connection to the outdoors.

FITTING THE KITCHEN TO THE HOUSE is what it's all about today. Contemporary kitchens are intimately connected to living and dining areas—and to the outdoors. Here, an opening provides a subtle separation between kitchen and sitting areas without impeding the flow of people and views.

UP-TO-DATE kitchen layouts are determined primarily by the placement of the three major elements—sink, range, and refrigerator—but should make room for today's secondary players, such as a food-prep sink and a microwave.

EATING IN THE KITCHEN or very near it keeps cooks out of isolation and allows diners to observe kitchen wizardry.

STYLE has as much to do with the "look" of a kitchen as it has to do with a historical period. Here, huge pine logs give a sense of the rustic, while frame-and-panel cabinet doors display their Craftsman style.

KITCHEN ISLANDS provide work space and storage space and buffer the open kitchen from the living areas.

SETTING THE STYLE

1 The rich materials in this kitchen renovation are reminiscent of 1940s California Spanish vernacular but are made contemporary by sleek, elegant detailing.

2 A renovated kitchen with quarter-sawn-oak cabinets suits its 1920s Arts and Crafts house yet still looks at home with stainless-steel appliances.

A style can mean a look that's homey, country, comfortable, or spare. Or a style can refer to a specific historical period and the details, colors, materials, and shapes that distinguish it. But such styles aren't cast in stone. For example, a cabinet brochure or kitchen magazine may tout a kitchen as Colonial without meaning that it's a reproduction kitchen like one in Williamsburg, Virginia. A modern house with casement windows can still have a Colonial-style kitchen.

On the following pages you'll find farmhouse kitchens, Shaker-style kitchens, Craftsman-style kitchens, and more. Some designers and homeowners are influenced by details found in vernacular houses, such as pale colors and thick, rounded-edge walls of Mediterranean houses, or the all-wood interior of a New England coastal cottage.

3 A kitchen for a large family gets its comfortable look from the Craftsman style, reflected in the frame-and-flat-panel cabinets and sage-green walls.

4 Textured ceramic tiles pick up on all the colors in this contemporary kitchen. Solid-surface counter-tops and light maple drawer faces complement darker, lavender-dyed upper cabinets with pierced beech inserts. Note the efficient layout of appliances and counterspace.

5 A new kitchen in an expanded farmhouse has Colonial-style raised-panel cabinets and 18th-century colors yet still has plenty of room for modern appliances, finishes, and kitchen gear.

1 A love for the Craftsman-style details of Greene and Greene influenced the cabinetry in this pine-log-framed kitchen in California.

2 This small and comfortable kitchen combines an old stove and traditional Shaker-style painted cabinets with a stainless-steel countertop and green-stained concrete floors.

Much of a kitchen's style comes from its cabinetry, particularly the doors. Lighting, flooring, wall covering, and appliances have a lesser effect, but if all the parts match, the style is enhanced. It's up to the homeowner whether a kitchen has a style that prevails down to the very last hinge. Function, technology, comfort, and the budget also play major roles, and, more often than not, kitchens are eclectic. Style mixes with style, material with material. A hand-rubbed wood cabinet stands next to a gleaming stainless-steel dishwasher. Even though Gustav Stickley, father of the American Craftsman style, called dark oak the flooring of choice, a Craftsman-style kitchen can have a tile floor or concrete floor. Some homeowners choose to disguise modern devices, but most accept the new beside the old. After all, our ancestors took advantage of new technology when it came their way.

3 Brightly painted cabinetry and whimsical shapes cheer up a family kitchen.

4 Stainless-steel cabinets with stainless-steel pulls and black granite countertops form an unmistakably contemporary kitchen.

5 Thick walls and plastered masonry found in Mediterranean houses are evoked in the deep-set shelves and plaster-veneer walls of this kitchen in coastal California.

1 A penchant for timber framing, a love for light, and a collection of Fiestaware dishes were the design springboards for a cheerful kitchen renovation.

2 In this cedar-framed gypsy wagon, dining is compact but comfortable. Table leaves are sycamore boards that slide into the bed frame. Brass refrigerator latches hold fast the cabinet doors. A small brass sink at left and a cast-iron wood-burning cookstove (not shown) round out the kitchen necessities.

3 A kitchen in the Pacific Northwest combines spare geometry and modern materials—concrete, concrete block, and steel—with a reverence for wood craftsmanship using native Douglas fir.

4 Diners can belly up to the counter or eat at the dining table in this colorful, contemporary kitchen with frameless plastic-laminate cabinets.

5 This 1930s New York apartment kitchen got a facelift back to its heyday. The restored range and a freestanding sink are vintage 1930s, as are factory lights and rectangular white-tile walls. The linoleum tile floor is a punchier version of a 1930s pattern.

Does style have an influence on a kitchen's layout? It can. The major players in the kitchen (refrigerator, sink, dishwasher, and cooking appliances) can still take the same positions from kitchen to kitchen, but they may be housed differently, depending on the style. A Craftsman-style kitchen might have built-in seating and cabinetry, or it may simply boast Craftsman-style doors. A contemporary kitchen often has banks of streamlined cabinets, with clean lines, minimal fuss, and high-tech materials.

To pin down the characteristics of individual historical styles, check For More Information in the back of this book (pp. 196-197). In the meantime, browse these kitchens for style ideas—traditional, contemporary, high-style, homestyle, freestyle, or a mix.

1 Texas vernacular-inspired details and family living gave rise to an open plan, including a children's play loft above the dining room. Materials were chosen with the environment in mind, including local southern yellow pine and cedar, water-based glues and finishes, and formaldehyde-free particleboard.

2 Frameless cabinets, cherry stripes, and sleek detailing give this kitchen renovation a contemporary look.

3 The rich color of the cherry cabinets in this kitchen is in striking contrast to the drywall partitions and exposed metal trusses in this bank turned private residence.

4 Cross-shaped pulls and contrasting white and dark finishes on these cabinets were inspired by the work of Charles Rennie Mackintosh, Scotland's famed Arts and Crafts designer.

UP-TO-DATE KITCHEN PLANS

No matter how great a kitchen looks, it's not much good if it doesn't work well. Good kitchens incorporate all the activities that their users require. Some people prefer a minimum of space so that they can prepare dinner efficiently and save money on kitchen finishes (kitchens cost more per square foot than any other room in the house). Others use the kitchen as a common room, with space for cooking, eating, laundry, homework, reading, and surfing the Net. The first step in planning a working kitchen is to list all activities. Then determine who will use the kitchen: One cook obviously requires less space than two, and sometimes whole families prepare meals together.

1

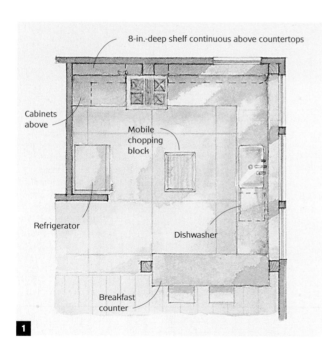

8-in.-deep shelf continuous above countertops

Cabinets above

Mobile chopping block

Refrigerator

Dishwasher

Breakfast counter

1

1 A 13-ft.-square kitchen allows just enough space for storage and food preparation without requiring a lot of walking back and forth. Base cabinets are extra deep to provide more storage.

2 A compact kitchen with Craftsman-style Douglas fir cabinets suits the cooking style of a retired couple on the California coast. The kitchen triangle takes a slight detour at the wall oven, which isn't used as often as the cooktop.

2

3 This small kitchen has it all: a compact working space, a refrigerator that's accessible without interfering with cooking, a place to sit, and a tall floor cabinet that conceals the mess but not the host.

4 A small service area with a rolling cart supplements the limited counterspace in an urban kitchen.

THE ACCESSIBLE KITCHEN

Most kitchens are designed for people who can stand, walk, and move with ease. But people are living longer, and people with physical disabilities are living independently. Many others suffer injuries that make it temporarily difficult to get around in tight spaces.

Whatever the disability, it is important to consider ease of operation when selecting not only appliances and hardware but also the layout for a new or renovated kitchen. And keep in mind that the equipment and design parameters that make a kitchen accessible for the disabled also make it easier to use for *everybody*.

Here's what to consider when designing an accessible kitchen. Keep the kitchen near to where groceries are unloaded, and make the paths between groceries and kitchen and kitchen and dining as straight and short as possible. Doorways should have a clear width of 32 in. (that means clear of the open door, too), and aisles should

be 42 in. wide. Because many kitchens have two cooks, make aisles wider, if possible. For a wheelchair, make a 5-ft. clear circle in the center. The kitchen triangle (see p. 20) must be larger than that in the traditional kitchen.

As in any two-cook kitchen, provide two work-space areas that are at least 36 in. wide each, and don't put them beside each other. One such work space should be 32 in. high and open underneath. In fact, provide work surfaces at several heights or configurations—one at 32 in., one at 36 in., and several with wheelchair room beneath them—and leave room on each side of appliances to set down food or cookware.

Locate most kitchen storage between 20 in. and 44 in. above the floor. Fixed shelves can make it harder to retrieve cookware and foodstuff, so consider pull-out shelves or drawers instead. A pantry works best with shallow shelves. In the hardware department, remember that levers and wide wire pulls are easier to use than knobs.

Locate electrical outlets beneath wall cabinets or specify a continuous plug molding along the backsplash or the wall-cabinet bottom to keep cords out of the way.

Keep the cooktop, sink, wall ovens, and microwave oven away from corners to allow each to be used from either side or from the front. Sinks can actually be adjustable in height, using flexible pipe connections. The easiest faucet to use is the single lever. A lower cooktop is helpful for someone in a wheelchair, and so is a microwave set at table height. The freezer in a side-by-side refrigerator model is easier to access than a freezer at the top or bottom.

Even windows require some thought. Keep operable windows within reach—not behind the cooktop. For a detailed source of accessible kitchen design, as well as accessible design for the rest of the house, see For More Information in the back of this book (pp. 196-197).

1 Spaces for letter writing, bill paying, and reading make for more livable kitchens.

2 This elegant work space in the kitchen contains the basics— a bookcase and desktop. The window is a bonus, both as a porthole and a design feature.

3 The striking figure of bubinga, also called African rosewood, makes kitchen cabinets that suit the bold styling and colors of a high-style Manhattan loft.

4 A tiny, dark-gray kitchen with a single window was transformed into a wide-open space (floor plan at right) with bold colors and plenty of light. Kitchen gear fits along one wall to provide clear floor space and easy access by a person in a wheelchair (above). Built-in seating provides a quiet corner to view both cooking and garden (left).

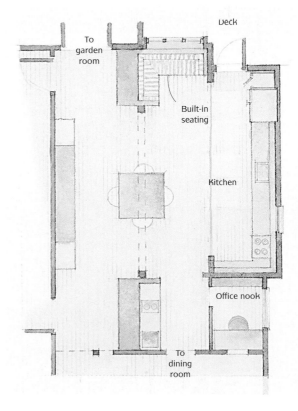

Deck

To garden room

Built-in seating

Kitchen

Office nook

To dining room

1 To make it handy for either a single cook or a whole crew, this kitchen has two zones: one with a compact triangle between refrigerator, sink, and cooktop, and a larger zone that includes a small kitchen table and a second sink (floor plan at right).

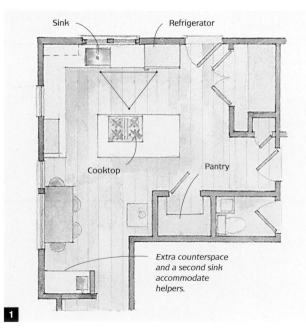

Sink

Refrigerator

Cooktop

Pantry

Extra counterspace and a second sink accommodate helpers.

1

Kitchen layouts depend on the placement of the three major elements: the refrigerator, sink, and cooking equipment. Each of these becomes a point in the famous kitchen work triangle, first put forth as kitchen gospel almost 50 years ago. This doctrine holds that the sink, refrigerator, and range should form the three points of a triangle, with set distances between them. These days, experts on kitchen planning think that the combined sum of the legs of the triangle should be no less than 15 ft. and no more than 22 ft. Some designers feel that a 12-ft. minimum can work, and others are willing to stretch it to 26 ft. Of the three legs, the distance between sink and cooktop should be the shortest—from 3 ft. to 6 ft.—not a bad idea when there's an 8-qt. pot full of boiled pasta to drain.

2 Cooking and clean-up areas are close together in this kitchen but exist in their own separate zones. A butcher-block island (on wheels) glides effortlessly between the two.

3 A raised counter at the perimeter of the wide countertop shields both kitchen wizardry and kitchen mess and accommodates spice storage. This handy work space is also close to the cooktop.

4 A kitchen for a retired couple is sized for one cook but allows for visits from children and grandchildren, who have easy access to the refrigerator.

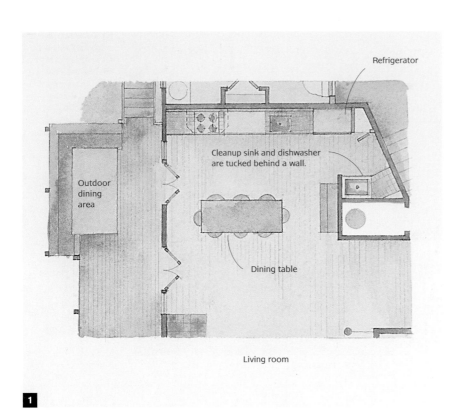

Refrigerator

Cleanup sink and dishwasher
are tucked behind a wall.

Outdoor
dining
area

Dining table

Living room

1

1

1 Cook before a
crowd but hide those
dirty dishes. An open-
plan kitchen (floor
plan above) meant for
group cooking (right)
keeps the messier
dishwashing zone
(above right) away
from direct view
of diners.

1

2 A small country kitchen is made cozier by a little bench, which suits one person with a cup of coffee.

For the cook who always goes solo, a galley kitchen (two rows of cabinetry and appliances) with a 38-in.-wide aisle is ideal. Two cooks require more room. A wide galley kitchen with an island or an L-shaped or U-shaped kitchen with an island provides more space for food preparation and more complex traffic patterns. Here, aisles should be 42 in. to 60 in. wide, depending on whether the island is also used for eating.

For families and serious cooking duos, two sinks are a blessing, if not already a necessity. Locate trash and recycling receptacles away from the main work areas so that one cook doesn't have to move each time vegetable scraps go in the compost bin. Consider tucking a sink and dishwasher into a corner to make a mini-scullery.

LAUNDRY IN THE KITCHEN?

Depending on your point of view, laundry facilities in or near the kitchen can be a blessing or a curse. On the plus side, if you have something on the stove, it's easier to keep tabs on laundry if it's nearby. For a house with serious gardeners or a passel of muddy kids, it's ideal if the laundry is near the mudroom *and* the kitchen. Keep a clean stash of clothes in the laundry, dump dirty clothes into the washer, wash in the laundry sink, put on fresh clothes, and head straight to the kitchen for lunch. Down in the basement is fine, too, if it's easy to access from the kitchen.

Less convenient is a washer or dryer set into the cabinetry of the kitchen proper. This setup was common in the 1950s and is sometimes the only solution in tight kitchens, but it disturbs the flow of kitchen work, especially if there's more than one cook. You may have seen washers or dryers hidden by a flip-up countertop; if you do laundry often, you'll find that such a design renders the countertop useful only as a lid, never for preparing food.

EATING IN THE KITCHEN

1 The raised floor and lowered ceiling of a breakfast nook create a cozy space.

2 There's room for one or two at this pull-out table in a small urban kitchen.

3 Peeled-log poles flank a countertop for informal meals in this Canadian island house.

1 This Arts and Crafts–style breakfast nook borrows space from the stud wall for a recessed bookshelf.

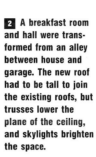 **2** A breakfast room and hall were transformed from an alley between house and garage. The new roof had to be tall to join the existing roofs, but trusses lower the plane of the ceiling, and skylights brighten the space.

3 A lowered countertop at the end of an island provides room for two diners.

4 A bump-out in the south wall provides extra space for a small eating area and allows the glancing sun in for breakfast.

5 A booth for two is built into the concrete-block wall of a 1950s desert-house addition.

6 A small table just this side of a bank of cabinets makes a comfortable place to work or eat without taking up valuable kitchen space.

1 Nothing is as welcoming as a sunny booth for breakfast, and an ideal spot is just out of the way of kitchen activity.

2 Breakfast in this retro-style kitchen is served at a 1950s-style chrome-and-plastic-laminate dinette set.

3 In a Prairie-style house on a Hawaiian ranch, a built-in bench and table offer views of rolling hills, distant volcanoes, and the ocean beyond.

4 A diner-style built-in booth complete with coat hooks and a jukebox serves as the "formal" dining space at the edge of the kitchen.

4

5

5 A lowered countertop in back of the island sink is the perfect place for a quick snack in this contemporary kitchen.

INFORMAL EATING SPACES

Many of us like to eat breakfast, lunch, and informal dinners near or in the kitchen, and some take all meals in the kitchen. But how to squeeze in that eating space? For starters, turn part of a peninsula or island countertop into a diner-style counter, with space below for stools. Another solution is to leave space for a small table and chairs in a part of the kitchen that won't see much traffic (try to keep the refrigerator and informal dining areas fairly close), or to build

the kitchen around a big farmhouse-style table that can serve as work space and eating/homework/gathering space. To add to an existing kitchen, consider closing in an outdoor space such as a breezeway or porch to make a breakfast room. Or assign the window end of a kitchen to dining, whether it's around a table or at built-in seating.

A built-in bench in or next to the kitchen can actually be the most sought-after seat in the house. The Spanish

version of the saying, "there's always room for one more," translates to "where six can eat, seven can." That's literally the situation with a *sitzbank*, the bank of benches that lines a traditional Austrian country kitchen—with a table pulled up for meals. Consider rounding the corners of the table that serves the sitzbank to make it easier to slip in and out. Just keep in mind that the person in the middle will always be the one who needs to get out first.

KITCHEN ISLANDS

1 A small kitchen island with a prep sink backs onto an informal dining table painted to match the room's cheery decor.

2 A small pull-out cart with a maple top and storage below comes out from under the counter when the heat is really on, while a purchased butcher-block table rolls around the kitchen for daily cooking.

3 A custom-built, quartersawn-oak table built to countertop height serves as a work-space island in a narrow kitchen. The table is easy to move, if needed.

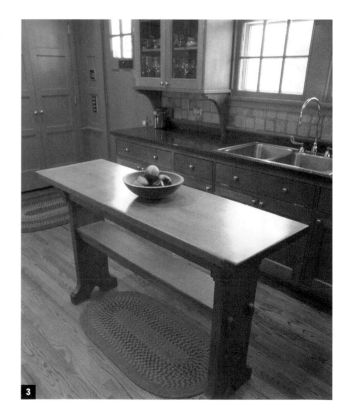

4 Kitchen islands don't have to be big or loaded with appliances. This slender island provides unencumbered work space with an overhang and room for two at the far end.

5 Multiple countertop heights make the island in this stylish kitchen addition quite versatile.

1 A workhorse island in the kitchen of a serious cook has no doors or drawers, so gear is easy to reach.

2 This raised countertop allows room for eating and sitting and also shields the cooktop behind.

4 This rolling island provides storage on two sides and a slightly lower than usual butcher-block countertop for preparing foods and kneading dough.

3 A generous kitchen island accommodates extra storage space, a prep sink, and a crown of cookware. The green-stained cabinets provide a colorful counterpoint to the white perimeter cabinetry.

2 A petite island of quartersawn oak with bottom-hinged storage bins and a large drawer has just enough countertop for chopping vegetables or rolling out pie crust.

1 The old kitchen table still serves its purpose as work space and gathering place.

THE ISLAND RETURNS

The not-so-new kid on the block is the kitchen island, progeny of the big work table that sat in the middle of the medieval kitchen, the Colonial kitchen, the turn-of-the-century English kitchen, and the farmhouse kitchen. An island these days serves the age-old purpose of making more work space, but it also serves a more modern purpose of buffering cooks from observers or kitchen from living space.

Most islands are rooted to the ground, even if they look like furniture. Building codes require electrical outlets on fixed islands, and it may suit the kitchen to build the outlets into design features. Task lighting for the island is normally provided by fixtures mounted on the ceiling. Any appliances located in

the island will require a hookup: electrical for a microwave oven or warming oven; gas for a range, oven, or cooktop; or water for a sink.

Carefully consider any appliances that you locate in the island, especially those that break up the counterspace. Cooktops on the island require a clear space *on three sides* to keep both children and grown-ups away from hot pots and spattering food. At least 15 in. is recommended on each side of the cooktop to act as landing spaces for hot pots. Heat-proof materials are essential, whether as countertop material or in the form of hot plates.

A sink in the island is handy for washing vegetables and filling pots, especially if it's off to one side. But a big clean-up sink with a dishwasher will guarantee that the island will be frequently littered with dirty dishes. If the island is the only place for a clean-up sink, a raised countertop can both hide the mess and make an ideal serving counter. If a giant island is part of the plan, don't place it between two major work areas, such as between the refrigerator and sink. In that case, consider breaking the island in two for clear passage.

It could be that the perfect island is slim, unencumbered by appliances and gizmos, and just the correct size for staging a buffet, drying homemade pasta, cooling pans of cookies, or making strudel. Islands can also have countertops of varying heights to accommodate different activities, such as eating, making pastry, and preparing vegetables.

Broad, simple, and not necessarily level, the farmhouse kitchen table still holds a lot of charm. If all that's required is work space (with no appliances or fittings other than a good, broad surface) and the space below isn't required for built-in storage, consider a table rather than an island. A table is more flexible. It works for serving meals as well as

for making pastry or bread, where its lower surface allows for more leverage in kneading or rolling dough.

For smaller spaces or for maximum flexibility, design a table that's easy to move, or buy one on wheels. Another inspiration for good-looking and functional (but not lightweight!) kitchen tables is the workbench. Antique workbenches can be used as furniture and easily serve the rest of their days as kitchen islands. Or let their sturdiness, joinery, and clever detailing inspire the design of a new kitchen island.

3

3 A wheeled cart tucks into one end of a big stationary island, ready for transporting food to the dining room. The tablecloth-like maple side is fixed in place, but the ends hinge up to make handles. The island cabinetry is curly maple; the legs are cherry.

4

4 This island in a family kitchen boasts a sink, knife storage, countertop seating, and dish-towel racks and is crowned by a massive pot rack.

FITTING THE KITCHEN TO THE HOUSE

A kitchen contains more gear than any room in the house, and it sees the most action. The North American kitchen has not always been the center of attention in the house (see the sidebar on p. 44), but today's kitchen is in the spotlight as never before. In new construction, it's a rare kitchen that is in a room of its own without at least an eating space and a few visual connections to other spaces. In older houses, space and budget constraints and aesthetics may keep the kitchen in a room to itself, and professional cooks and serious amateurs may prefer that a kitchen not be part of a larger space. But even those who prefer keeping folks out of their kitchens welcome an audience on the other side of a peninsula or at least far enough away so that they don't get in the cook's way.

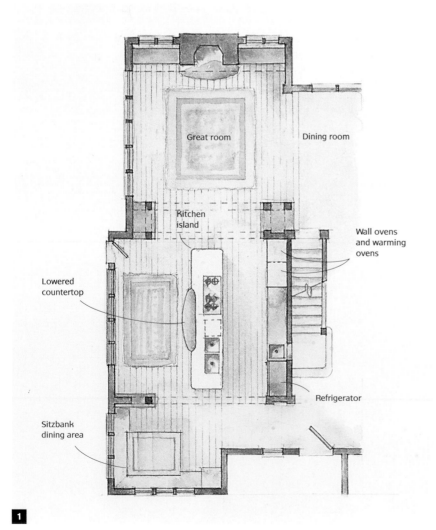

Great room

Dining room

Kitchen island

Wall ovens and warming ovens

Lowered countertop

Refrigerator

Sitzbank dining area

1

1

1 This kitchen is open to living and built-in seating areas on each end, but its boundaries are staked out by arched soffits and trimmed openings. There's plenty of circulation around the kitchen (floor plan facing page), leaving space for a cook to work efficiently without cross traffic.

1 What better way to celebrate the entrance to the most important room in the house than with a pergola?

2 The designer/ owner of this kitchen found a peninsula/ breakfast bar to be a diplomatic way to keep noncooks at a safe distance.

3 A large twin-tower divider separates the kitchen from the living room while sharing light and sound between the two.

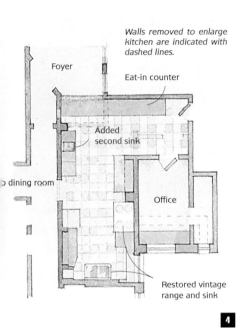

Walls removed to enlarge kitchen are indicated with dashed lines.

Foyer

Eat-in counter

Added second sink

o dining room

Office

Restored vintage range and sink

4

4 **4**

4 To make an informal eating area in the kitchen, 3 ft. were borrowed from the foyer of a 1930s apartment (floor plan at left). A slot in the new wall allows light and air to circulate and guides guests to the kitchen (left). Also greeting guests is a photo from the 1939 New York World's Fair (far left), an apt image for the food writer and photographer who live here.

5 A bank of cubbyholes atop the peninsula counter provides storage and shields any kitchen mess from diners.

5

1 The major spaces in this house are arranged around a central square that's lit from above by a cupola. The open kitchen also adds morning light to the house from its east-facing windows (floor plan below).

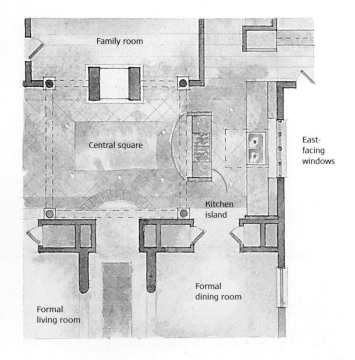

Family room

Central square

East-facing windows

Kitchen island

Formal dining room

Formal living room

1

2 From the entry of the house, there's a distant but tempting view of the kitchen framed with recycled Douglas fir timbers.

2

3 In this Craftsman-and-contemporary-blend house, the kitchen can be partly closed off by operable shutters between upper and base cabinets; lighting unites the spaces.

There's no shortage of ways to connect a kitchen visually and physically to the living or main dining areas yet keep the rooms separate. Opening the kitchen to the second floor allows the smell of breakfast cooking to waft up and the light from the rising sun to bounce down. For same-level connections, try the age-old pass-through, first used by servants and now a conduit for conversation, appetizers, whole meals, and dirty dishes. The size, shape, and detailing of the pass-through can vary, depending on the style of the house, the amount of stuff going back and forth, and the size of the budget.

Floor and wall cabinets, whether opaque or transparent, make fine buffers, as do open shelves. All provide convenient storage for dishes, especially if doors open from both the kitchen and dining room. The cabinets or shelves can be loaded directly from the dishwasher and unloaded directly from shelf to the table.

4 Even a kitchen that has clear-cut boundaries on its own level can be opened up to views and light from the floor above.

1 A freestanding kitchen workstation wraps its arms around the food-prep zone of a large kitchen (above left) and buffers the sink from a sitting area and bookshelves on the other side (above right).

2 A wide opening flanked by glass-paneled cabinets serves as a pass-through between a well-lit kitchen and dining area.

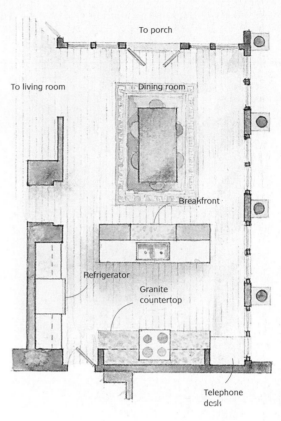

3 A freestanding breakfront cabinet affords the wash-up crew a view, while oak panels hide dirty dishes (above). Glazed upper cabinets, operable from both sides for convenience, allow light to pass between dining and kitchen areas. The exterior wall of the kitchen is filled with windows rather than cabinets (floor plan above right).

To porch

To living room

Dining room

Breakfront

Refrigerator

Granite countertop

Telephone desk

1 A narrow island provides the only physical and visual boundary for a small family kitchen. The exposed ceiling structure adds volume to the compact living/dining/cooking area.

A SLICE OF AMERICAN KITCHEN HISTORY

Many of us romanticize the American Colonial kitchen, with its massive center table, utensils hanging for ready use, and head-high fireplace in constant use. In this room, called the keeping room or common room, the family gathered to cook, eat, work, read, talk, play, and sometimes sleep. Larger early houses had a parlor on the other side of the fireplace and, in time, more rooms to the side or above. To signify increased gentility and financial status, families would gather, entertain, bathe, and sleep in the newer, and colder, rooms. By the mid-1850s, middle-class homes had separate kitchens and dining rooms so that flies and cooking smells (and servants) could be kept from diners. Even worse was the city kitchen of 100 years ago, which was in the cellar or at street level. Dark, wretched, and stuffy, the city kitchen was still the center of life for working classes and servants.

The kitchen was due for a change, however. One prominent reformer was Catharine Beecher, whose well-received books on domestic economy in the mid-1800s put forth the kitchen as the core

of the house, like a cook's galley in a steamship, efficient and within easy reach of common-use rooms: "Thus, the mother can have her parlor, nursery, and kitchen, all under her eye at once." Beecher foresaw that fewer families would be hiring domestics, so she promoted "economy of labor," which called for smaller homes, to save on steps and housework. Yet, the kitchen should not be too small; instead, Beecher urged that the largest and most pleasant rooms in the house be for common use as the kitchen, everyday parlor, and dining room. All three rooms could even be combined into one if space was limited (back to the Colonial keeping room!). A few decades later in his influential magazine, *The Craftsman*, Gustav Stickley promoted a return to bright, clean kitchens and the recombination of dining room and kitchen, likewise inspired by the Colonial kitchen.

At the same time, there was a move to streamline the kitchen for "scientific cookery." Within the fledgling field of home economics, it was believed that light, mild food cooked to uniform standards

in laboratory-like kitchens would produce a healthier population. This belief resulted from a new understanding of nutrition and hygiene, but it did little to improve the flavor and variety of the typical American meal, and it diluted (purposely) the flavors of immigrant cooking. One proponent of scientific cooking imagined clean, tightly run homes, cupboards full of machine-prepared, ready-to-heat or eat foods and—even better—a pneumatic tube that connected each kitchen with a central supply station. Factory-made food would be cleaner and more consistent, resulting in happy, healthy children, sober husbands, and more leisure time.

Technology was making this dream come true with devices such as dependable gas ranges, refrigerators, and factory-made cabinetry and food, all at the expense of the size and comfort of the kitchen. Families became smaller, too, and less likely to include three generations, further justifying smaller kitchens. Easy access to prepared food reduced the need for a pantry. Dining and living rooms were often designed

as one room, and the American kitchen shrank until there was just enough room for mom. While a good-sized kitchen might be 10 ft. square, many a kitchen shriveled enough to be proudly dubbed a kitchenette. At mid-century, the ideal meal was envisioned as not only instant but instantaneous, as served by television's futuristic Mrs. Jetson, who made whole dinners appear at the push of a button on her Food-a-Rac-a-Cycle. If she suffered as a housewife, it was not from slaving over a hot stove or from the present-day angst of having too many options. Do we cook, heat up, or eat out? What kind of salad greens to buy? Do we dare to eat an egg? Instead, Jane Jetson took to her bed with a sore wrist from pushing buttons.

The parents of baby boomers wanted to get out of the kitchen. Baby boomers, and their children, want to get back in. Beginning in the 1950s, the kitchen reversed its shrinking trend and often included an informal eating area. These days, the kitchen can include space to cook, eat, work, play, talk—everything but sleep. Sound familiar?

2 A compact kitchen with contrasting colors, textures, and materials fits neatly under the stairs in a corner of a studio flat in London. A small refrigerator and dishwasher are concealed behind the two walnut-paneled base cabinet doors to the left of the extra-deep single-bowl sink.

3 In an otherwise open living space, the kitchen is sheltered within gable ends that are tied together across the entrance.

4 In keeping with the period, this new Art Deco–style kitchen has a frosted-glass window in the swinging door to the dining room.

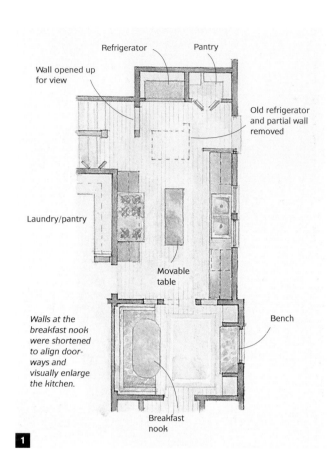

Wall opened up for view

Refrigerator

Pantry

Old refrigerator and partial wall removed

Laundry/pantry

Movable table

Walls at the breakfast nook were shortened to align doorways and visually enlarge the kitchen.

Bench

Breakfast nook

1

1

1 A little conjuring made this kitchen look bigger. Doorways between living room, breakfast nook, and kitchen were enlarged and aligned to give the kitchen more breathing room, making it seem larger and less isolated (floor plan above).

2 A wall of double-sided cabinets separates the family room from the kitchen without isolating the cook. The ends of the island are dropped to reduce its apparent size and to provide two working heights for different tasks.

2

At the open-plan end of the spectrum, the kitchen takes its place in a larger space, sometimes called the great room. You can shield the kitchen with an island or peninsula or bare the cabinets and countertops to anyone with a yen to chop onions. Even a kitchen that bares its countertops can still veil its baser aspects—namely the dishwashing area. For cooks who love to entertain but don't want help, make the kitchen walls at countertop height for conversation but keep the openings at a minimum.

Even if the ideal kitchen has no wall to speak of between the kitchen and the rest of the house, it's hard for a kitchen to pretend it's anything but a kitchen. The lighting is stronger, there's more bulk—cabinets, appliances, range hoods, dishes, pots and pans—and materials, colors, and textures will be different from the rest of the house.

3 In a converted warehouse, restaurant-size appliances and a countertop wide open to living and dining areas are designed for entertaining large groups of people.

CONNECTING TO THE OUTDOORS

1 A view of San Francisco Bay from the kitchen window makes the placement of this sink an excellent choice.

2 Expanses of glass to the east and south allow unrestricted views from this Seattle kitchen. To compensate for the amount of glass, steel cross bracing stabilizes the structure and evokes the form of both tree and treehouse.

3 During the summer, the door to a screened porch in a Massachusetts house is open for family dining from morning until bedtime.

Most kitchens benefit from a connection to the outdoors, whether by windows, doors, or both. Kitchens need light, ventilation, comfort, and proximity to the front or back door for bringing in groceries and, for a lucky few, taking lunch *alfresco*. And what cook doesn't appreciate a view? Balance the close-up view—where the kids play, where the birds feed, where the kitchen garden grows—with distant views of treetops, mountains, a skyscraper, or water. A kitchen doesn't even require an outside wall to get the view, as long as part of the kitchen faces a nearby window.

4 This kitchen peninsula is but one of four stretches of countertop in a small but comfortable kitchen, but it has the best view hands down.

1 A kitchen/family room looks out over a veranda and courtyard garden (floor plan below left). The kitchen ceiling follows the roof line to expose the Japanese-influenced timber frame, while corridors have flat ceilings. Windows are sturdier versions of *shoji* using sandblasted panels with removable wooden grids.

2 A bench just outside the kitchen door of this Arts and Crafts house is the perfect spot for the cook to take a breather.

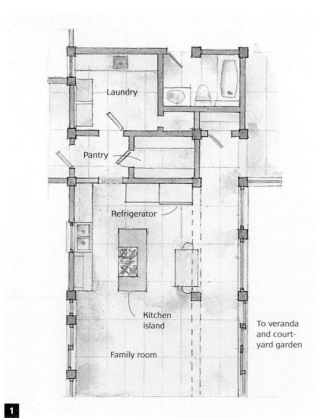

Laundry

Pantry

Refrigerator

Kitchen island

Family room

To veranda and court-yard garden

1

2

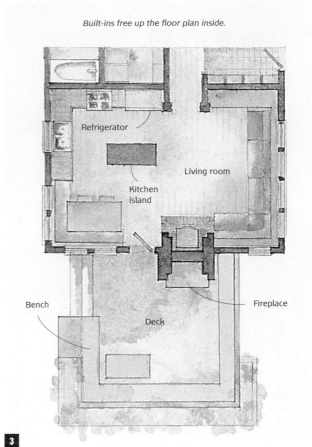

Built-ins free up the floor plan inside.

Refrigerator

Living room

Kitchen
island

Bench

Deck

Fireplace

3

4 A dumbwaiter hoists groceries from the garage below. With a cherry cabinet and an iron pulley showcased behind glass, it makes a handsome workhorse.

3 A massive brick fireplace is a popular gathering place for the family in this small house, where it's easy to bring meals from the kitchen for outdoor dining (floor plan above right).

DUMBWAITERS

If you plan to build on a hill-side, or if your kitchen is above ground level, consider including a dumbwaiter in your kitchen. A residential-style dumbwaiter carries a small load between 65 lb. and 150 lb. Cab sizes (the box that holds contents) range from 2 ft. square to 3 ft. square. Commercial dumbwaiters are often the same size but of sturdier construction and can carry up to 500 lb. Hand-operated dumb-waiters, which are less expensive and require less maintenance, are operated by a rope; an automatic brake kicks in when you stop pulling. Electric dumbwaiters operate by call buttons and may fall under the elevator code for construction and installation—check your building department for local standards. The machinery takes up the same room (2 ft. to 4 ft.) for each type of dumb-waiter, but it can be located below the dumbwaiter on an electric model, whereas manual machinery is always at the top of the hoistway.

4

1 This kitchen juts out from the main portion of a coastal house to take in a dramatic view of a granite ledge and the roiling sea.

2 A Wyoming kitchen opens up to the sunny south but is buffered from the cold north wall by a bank of three small rooms—a utility room containing refrigerator and recycling, a pantry, and the laundry (to the right in the photo).

3 In one of several shaded breezeways around an Arizona house, the homeowners take advantage of a grill and a prep sink set in a stainless-steel countertop on a split-face concrete-block base (left). Dinner *alfresco* is served on a thick wood table that cantilevers from a cast-in-place concrete wall (right). Indoor meals are eaten on the other half of the table.

4 A screened dining/sitting porch just off the kitchen is one of the most-used rooms in an energy-efficient house in Texas.

CABINETS

Of all the elements in a kitchen, cabinets most set the tone for the entire room. They dictate the style, determine how well the kitchen works, take up much of the floor space, and eat up the lion's share of the budget. It makes sense to understand where cabinets come from, how they're made, and what goes inside them.

To start, take a look at style. There's no design decree for cabinet style these days, and that can be both daunting and exhilarating. Cabinet heights, colors, hardware, and door and drawer configurations can be mixed within the same kitchen to benefit both style and function. Hardworking, good-looking cabinets can come from a cabinet factory, from a one-person shop, or from anywhere in between. Together, these sources turn out an astonishing variety of finishes, sizes, and styles.

Learn about cases, understand how door and drawer types relate to case types, and discover how many options are available for doors and drawers: solid, transparent, paneled, flat, laminated, painted, carved, and more. Cabinets can fool the eye, but look closely at the construction of a door or drawer to assess how well it will hold up. Cabinet hardware adds the finishing touch and helps set the stage for a smoothly working kitchen. Finally, look inside the cabinets to discover the amazing array of accessories that can make your final choice of cabinets work better and more efficiently.

TRIMMING CABINET tops and bottoms contributes more to style and function than it might seem. Cabinets can stop short of the ceiling or go all the way up; cabinet bottoms may meet the floor or incorporate a toespace.

DOORS AND DRAWERS tell the most about kitchen style. Here, painted door panels and drawer faces frame a black-slate countertop and backsplash. Drawn-glass panels add contrast to the upper cabinets.

CABINET HARDWARE can transform a kitchen. Pulls, hinges, drawer slides, and specialized accessory hardware make an enormous difference in how cabinets work and look and how much they cost.

CASES FOR CABINETS can have face frames, or they can be frameless (like these). Choosing a case type and selecting doors and hardware go hand in hand.

ELEMENTS OF STYLE

1 Curves enliven a wall cabinet and set it apart from rectilinear base cabinets with square-edged countertops. To add contrast, base cabinets are stained and wall cabinets painted; butt hinges and button pulls unify the design.

2 These Italian-made custom-manufactured frameless cabinets feature paneled doors and flat-front drawers.

3 Frameless, walnut-paneled cabinets and a bank of large and sturdy drawers frame a five-burner stove in a London studio kitchen that's cleverly tucked under the stairs. Drawers in the toekick area make the most of the limited space.

Each element of a cabinet contributes to its style. The case is the basic box, and how it is built gives the cabinet its initial identity. *Face-frame* cabinets are the traditional style in the United States and are still the most common; *frameless* cabinets were developed in Europe in the 1950s to speed production and to conserve wood. A face-frame cabinet has a flat frame that covers the exposed edges of the box (see the drawing on p. 64). Doors and drawers may either be set into the frame or overlay it (see the drawings on p. 69). Inset doors are more painstaking to make and hang than overlay doors, but they are standard in historical styles. A frameless cabinet is a simple box, and its doors and drawers, which are just a hair's breadth apart, nearly cover the case completely.

2 Curvaceous contemporary cabinets are trimmed with a strip of fused dichroic glass and fitted with matching brushed-nickel and glass pulls.

1 The client/father of the architect built these face-frame cabinets from native walnut, with flat drawers over flat-paneled doors. Wall cabinets have sand-blasted glass panels.

3 Lavender upper cabinets and maple lower cabinets (all frameless) set the style in this streamlined modern kitchen.

4 Pleasing proportions and simple, flat detailing are the hallmarks of a Shaker-style cabinet.

Kitchen cabinets can come from many sources, from a one-person shop to a huge factory. No matter who makes the cabinets, before you place an order, make sure that you have plans and elevations of the cabinetry for *your* kitchen and ask for—or prepare for yourself—a list that calls out each cabinet, its accessories, and hardware.

You can buy manufactured cabinets through a home center, lumberyard, kitchen-products dealer, contractor, or designer. The cabinets can be installed by the dealer, a contractor, or the homeowner. They are built as components, which makes them easier to move than built-in cabinets, although filler pieces may be required to cover gaps between cabinet carcases, especially in stock cabinets. Manufactured cabinets are available at three levels, starting with stock cabinets, which offer a fixed selection of sizes, styles, finishes, hardware, and accessories. Stock cabinets aren't made in nonstandard sizes or finishes and are available off the shelf or within two to four weeks at the longest. Understandably, they're about half the cost of many custom-manufactured cabinets.

Semicustom and custom manufacturers offer a fixed but wide range of styles, finishes, hardware, accessories, sizes, and configurations but may custom-make some pieces. Quality is generally very good to premium; delivery takes 2 to 12 weeks. Semicustom cabinets have fewer available options and cost about 25% less than cabinets from custom manufacturers. All reputable manufacturers and dealers offer reliable quality control and follow-through services.

A cabinetmaker or millwork shop builds custom cabinets to specifications. An experienced cabinetmaker can offer the most design flexibility and can handle a wide range of sizes, materials, finishes, hardware, and configurations. Shop-built cabinets also can be built in larger sections to fit site-measured situations. Cabinets are delivered and installed from about 6 to 20 weeks after the order. The shop will install the cabinets. Shop-built cabinets are usually of high quality, but it's essential to ask the cabinetmaker for references and for you to provide detailed specifications.

Knocked-down (KD) or ready-to-assemble (RTA) cabinet parts are an option for the fairly handy. KD cabinets are available from large retailers such as IKEA. Mail-order houses use the term RTA and often sell components only to cabinetmakers or contractors. Components are put together by the homeowner or a hired carpenter. This alternative allows for mixing and matching of hardware, styles, and colors, and it can be economical—if the cabinet design is not complicated, cases are frameless, dimensions are standard, ordering is precise, and the builder has some experience. Materials and joinery equal those found in manufactured cabinets, but how they are assembled can't be controlled in the factory.

5 A freestanding sideboard blends seamlessly with the cherry cabinets in this Arts and Crafts–style kitchen.

1 Frameless cabinets with medium-density fiberboard (MDF) panels take on a traditional look, thanks to molding applied to the doors.

2 A galley kitchen in an energy-efficient house gets down to basics with cabinet doors and drawer fronts left off for economy and utility.

3 An old pharmaceutical cabinet finds new life as a base for a breakfast counter in a new timber-frame house.

How cabinets fit into a kitchen is another factor in understanding style. It may be the memory of the old homestead with its country kitchen and accompanying smells of home-cooked food, or it may be nostalgia for a supposedly simpler, warmer time, but many of today's kitchens are taking on the look of the "unfitted" kitchen of our ancestors. Someone's grandmother might recall a farmhouse kitchen from the 1920s as having a Hoosier cabinet, lots of open shelves, a pantry, a dish cupboard, a freestanding range, a pedestal sink, and a big kitchen table. Our present-day unfitted look can include cabinets of different finishes and styles, countertops of varying heights and materials, freestanding cabinets, and open shelves. Even built-in cabinetry can take on an unfitted look by acquiring legs and crown molding.

4

4 There are no wall cabinets on the window wall in this coastal house, but a blue valance rail continues the line of the dish rack and shelves beside the range hood. The bright blue reflects the owner's love for Greek folk architecture. Large drawers on the dining side hold tableware and children's toys.

5 An elegant kitchen in a renovated house contrasts the clean lines of simple painted wood cabinets and stainless-steel countertops and range with the texture of a tile backsplash, distressed cherry island cabinets, and a rough limestone floor. Doors are frame and panel, and drawers are one piece; all are inset into face-frame cases.

5

1 The cabinets in this farmhouse-kitchen addition are Art Deco–inspired, with details such as a slick, off-white painted finish, streamlined pulls, and vision glass on the upper cabinets. The frames above the cabinets contain a rotating gallery of the homeowner's artwork.

2 Timber-frame aesthetics meet Craftsman-style cabinets in this California house. Reclaimed longleaf pine, which is dense and stable, is abundant in floors, cabinets, and trim.

CABINET DIMENSIONS

Designers are rethinking cabinet dimensions. For years, the standard wall cabinet has been placed 16 in. to 18 in. above the countertop, but for a serious cook, or a tall one, this may not be high enough. More suitable may be a wall cabinet 24 in. above the countertop or even no wall cabinets at all, replaced instead by open shelves or a separate pantry, especially if the look is traditional. (Wall cabinets over sinks should be at least 30 in. above the countertop.)

The opposite tack is to drop the wall cabinet all the way to the countertop, making a china-cabinet-like connection to the base cabinet. Researchers say that the most useful storage space is between hip height and shoulder height, so the occasional china cabinet may be more

suitable than ordinary cabinets. Just note that a kitchen with a lot of wall cabinets will benefit from the structural support of a layer of ½-in. plywood under the drywall.

Also consider the height of base cabinets. Standard base cabinets are 34½ in. high to allow for a 1½-in.-thick countertop and a 36-in.-high work surface. Again, the tall cook won't find this a comfortable height for all kitchen tasks (6-ft.-plus-tall Julia Child has 38-in.-high counters). Bakers may want to *drop* part of the countertop to 32 in. for ease of kneading and rolling out pastry. Ten years ago it wasn't easy to specify an odd-height cabinet, but today it's possible to get cabinets that are taller or shorter to fit the task or the cook.

Cabinet depths can vary, too, but it's best to go for shallower rather than deeper. The standard wall cabinet is 15 in. deep, but a 10-in. or 12-in. upper cabinet may suit you better: It won't get in the way of a tall or an active cook yet will still hold most glassware and dishes (just be sure you have clearance for your own dishware by giving your cabinet designer actual dimensions of items to be stored). If you like deep countertops—say 30 in.—you can special-order extra-deep base cabinets. A less expensive option is to install a standard 24-in.-deep base cabinet so that it is 4 in. to 5 in. proud of the wall. The countertop will cover the gap in the back, but be sure to specify extra-deep panels for any exposed cabinet sides so that there won't be a gap between cabinet and wall.

3 This breakfront was designed to conceal an oven and a microwave oven/vent. The corner unit has a flip-down surface that hides small appliances.

4 The cabinets in this tiny kitchen in a Minnesota cabin can be wrapped up in a larger cabinet; the design is inspired by Norwegian architecture.

5 A seashore aesthetic inspired the "catch of the day" blackboard and sea-worn cabinets, which are painted-and-rubbed pine with beaded-inset doors and stainless-steel hardware.

CASE BASICS

1

2

1 Face-frame case edges are beaded, while drawers are plain front and doors are frame and beaded panel.

2 Frameless cabinets, which can be more time-consuming and exacting to make than face-frame cabinets, can take on a traditional style with paneled doors and drawers. These cabinets have birch-plywood cases and lacquered solid cherry doors and drawers.

FRAMELESS AND FACE-FRAME CASES

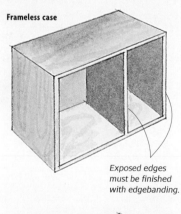

Frameless case

Exposed edges must be finished with edgebanding.

Face-frame case

Exposed edges are covered with flat frame.

3

3 Frameless cases have no frame on front, so doors and drawers can be wider than on traditional face-frame cases.

4 Frameless cabinet cases are fitted with traditional-looking doors and simple one-piece drawers. The doors, with their beadboard panels and flat frames, give the cabinets an Adirondack-style look.

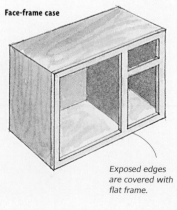

4

5 The designer of this kitchen preferred frameless cabinets for their accessibility but took inspiration for doors and drawers from Arts and Crafts designer Charles Rennie Mackintosh. Cabinets are solid African mahogany and mahogany plywood; portions are painted with several coats of white lacquer, which maintains the texture of the grain.

6 The cabinets on the breakfront have simple, Shaker-style flat-panel oak-veneer doors inset into the face frame. All doors have butt hinges and tapered 1-in. block pulls. Inset drawer fronts are solid oak.

7 Face frames are painted a pale, warm gray, drawer and doors are finished clear, and pulls are white porcelain for subtle contrast. Most of the countertop is plastic laminate with wood edge trim; a butcher-block surface sits behind the lunch counter.

DOORS & DRAWERS

1 Doors and drawers determine the cabinet style. Custom Shaker-style cabinetry makes good use of simple doors and a few small drawers—note the column of drawers in the island and two small drawers below the doors in the upper cabinets. All cabinetry is cherry, and the countertop is granite tile.

2 Built to last, these cherry drawers (above) boast dovetailed corner joints and open on wood runners for quiet operation. Black wire pulls are integrated into black-enamel-painted horizontal bead trim. The top panels have one, then two beads, and the bottom drawers each have three rows of beading. The top three panels are not drawers but act as the public face of a backsplash (above right).

3 These inset cabinet doors have vertical-ribbed vision glass (also called obscure glass) inserted in the frames. Shelves are fixed at the same level in all the wall cabinets.

1 A wide-angle view of the woods was worth more than wall-cabinet storage space in this Puget Sound kitchen. The lower cabinets have the simplest of door types—reveal overlay with finger pulls.

2 Panel doors can acquire character simply with the addition of beading. Beading with a dark reveal adds depth to a flat-panel maple door with a flat frame (top). A reveal-overlay door of stained and glazed maple has roped beading around the panel (bottom).

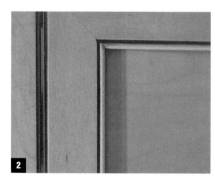

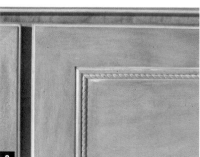

3 Cabinet door stiles and rails are typically butt-jointed and occasionally mitered; the cabinet-maker gave a subtle twist to these ash cabinets by using a quail-tail joint. The countertop is maple.

4 The faux-leather look on the door panels in this cottage kitchen was achieved with paint and glazes. Inset lower drawers have basket cases.

5 Reveal-overlay frame-and-panel doors and drawers acquire a warm red color from aniline dye. The color blends with the red-brown-stained concrete floor and makes a quiet contrast to the lighter hemlock beadboard wainscoting.

A GALLERY OF DOORS

6 If doors are inset into a face-frame cabinet, the frame of the cabinet (shaded area) is fully visible (A). Reveal overlay doors show part of the frame (B). Frameless cabinets take flush ovcrlay doors, which are just a hair's breadth apart (C).

Single-piece door

Beadboard or edge-glued planks

Molding applied to single-piece door

A

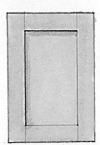

Frame and panel

Beaded frame and panel

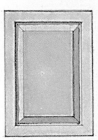

Raised panel

B

Glass panel

Beadboard panel

Bin door
(hinged at bottom)

C

1 A fir cabinet, known as the "cake-display cupboard" by the architect and homeowner, adds storage yet allows light into the room. Drawers overlay the face-frame cabinet below.

2 Inspired by New England frame-and-panel construction and the design vernacular of the High Plains, the cabinetmaker hand-carved the door panel then applied the oil-based paint. Hinges are simple, square-cornered butt hinges. The pull is hand-forged iron.

3 Wire panel doors provide texture with a view in an island cabinet. On each side of the banks of inset drawers is molding special-ordered from a local fabricator and applied by the cabinet manufacturer.

4 Pots and pans are out of sight but easily retrieved in extra-large drawers under the cooktop in a West Coast house.

4

Swinging cabinet doors may look traditional, but sliding doors are the door of choice in restaurant kitchens, where it's imperative to keep the way clear for heads and shins. Sliders can be real space savers in small kitchens, too. On the downside, sliding doors require tracks at the top and bottom of the case opening, and the tracks need to be kept clean. And sliders don't allow full access to a cabinet, since one half is always covered by the doors. But don't cling to the thought that sliding doors just aren't traditional: Modern (1950s) architecture, which championed the sliding cabinet door, is now looked upon with nostalgia, and its artifacts are certifiable antiques.

Other alternatives to the swinging door are pocket doors, flipper doors, and tambour doors. Flipper doors are inset and pivot and slide into the cabinet, so they take up room in the cabinet. They're common on appliance garages or on cabinetry that holds electronic equipment. Tambour doors, assembled from narrow slats on a flexible backing, are also common on appliance garages and electronic cabinets for the same reason: They stay out of the way when open.

5 The curved cabinets in this island have medium-density fiberboard (MDF) panels with solid wood trim. MDF is easier to curve than wood and takes paint well.

5

1 The doors to these maple wall cabinets sandwich a sandblasted pattern between laminated-glass panels. This gives the effect of sandblasted glass without showing blotches when the panels are touched by wet or greasy fingers.

2 Patterned obscure glass panels break up cabinet contents into abstract patterns and colors. The frame-less lower cabinets are maple.

3 Drawers are traditionally simpler than doors. A one-piece drawer front (bottom right) is not expensive to build and may be suitable for light loads. It is not as strong and long-lasting as a two-piece front (top right).

DRAWER TYPES

Single-piece drawer over frame-and-panel door

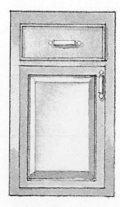

Beaded-edge drawer over frame-and-raised-panel door

Ungraduated bank of drawers

Graduated bank of drawers

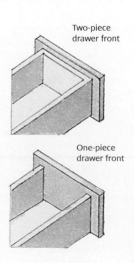

Two-piece drawer front

One-piece drawer front

4 A glass-fronted slot on each drawer allows a layer of pasta or grains to provide color and pattern to the cabinets.

6 The corners of these Douglas fir frameless doors are notched to act as negative pulls and to add texture and color to the composition. Behind the notches is a block of aniline-dyed bird's-eye maple, which hides cabinet contents.

5 The middle door panel is wire mesh, while the left, flat-panel inset maple doors are handrubbed with several colors of paint to achieve an antique finish. Hardware is a coiled iron pull. Tiny drawers below the door contain spices and kitchen gadgets.

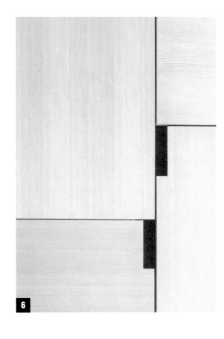

HARDWARE

1 An inset steel grid provides a finger pull for a Douglas fir cabinet. Turning the grain direction from door to door accentuates the figure of the wood.

2 Super-long wire pulls add a design accent and provide easy access to doors and drawers.

3 Ceramic door pulls share the job with whimsical pewter animals in this 1950s retro kitchen.

GALLERY OF PULLS AND LATCHES

Bin pull

Recessed pull

File-drawer pull

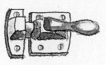
Icebox latch

Wire pull

Pull and escutcheon

Colonial knob

Cupboard latch

Iron pull

Pendant pull

Marble knob

Twisted iron pull

Flush pull

Porcelain knob

H-latch

4

DRAWER SLIDES

Drawers may or may not have pulls, but they always have slides (also called glides). Today the majority of drawers are fitted with side-mounted epoxy-coated (for reduced noise) steel slides and nylon rollers. Less expensive slides are mounted at the corner of the drawer, while heavy-duty slides fit on the side. Heavy-duty ball bearings last longer and are more stable than nylon rollers, but they also cost more. Full-extension slides add to the cost, but many designers automatically specify them because they expose the contents of the entire drawer to view when opened. To save money, consider using full-extension slides on just the top drawers. Drawer slides also may be self-closing; these shut automatically when they're 3 in. or 4 in. from a closed position.

Side-mounted metal slides are a recent innovation, so for historical authenticity go for either undermounted slides or wood slides. Undermounted drawer slides are more expensive, especially if you want full extension, and although they take up some of the depth of the available drawer space, they are invisible and allow for smooth-sliding drawers. A few cabinetmakers still make wood slides that run in wood slots in the drawer sides because they prefer traditional looks and silent operation.

5

1 Polished-brass button pulls finish the top of a china base cabinet. Door frames are quartersawn white oak. They were oiled and then topped off with semigloss clear lacquer.

2 These unusual pigmented urethane pulls were cast in a silicone mold formed by cow vertebrae.

3 Brushed-nickel and glass pulls set off a bank of contemporary cabinets.

4 Rugged aluminum-angle pulls fit in with the other materials in a Southwest house: Douglas fir countertops, concrete floor, and rammed-earth walls.

5 Face-mounted hinges are easy to install but cannot be adjusted, while butt hinges usually require a mortise and are difficult to adjust. Some adjustment is possible with pivot hinges; concealed cup hinges are very easy to adjust.

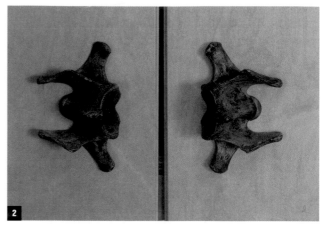

GALLERY OF HINGES

Face-mounted hinges

Self-closing offset

Flush

Butterfly

Ball tip

Butt hinges

Steeple-tip split hinge

Olive

Pivot or knife hinge

Concealed cup hinge

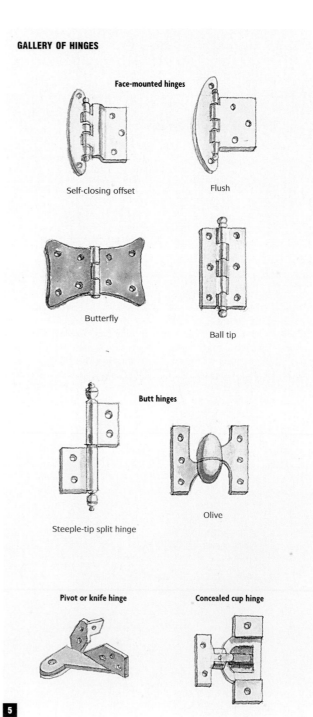

6

6 Cheery colors and a zigzag table leg are balanced by a dark slate backsplash and countertop and by the rhythm of long, steel pulls used both vertically and horizontally.

HINGES

7 Fanciful bronze pulls brighten dark-green-stained frameless cabinets.

Hinges are the supporting actors in cabinetry hardware. They don't get star billing like pulls, but most cabinet doors wouldn't work without them. The European cabinet revolution in the 1950s that brought us frameless cabinets also brought the concealed cup hinge, a complicated-looking hinge that allows a cabinet door to be easily adjusted, both during installation and years later, when a door might have sagged. These days, concealed adjustable hinges are also available for face-frame cabinets. Larger concealed hinges may require a mounting block on the inside of the face frame. A more expensive but cleaner detail is to run the mounting block the full vertical length of the inside of the face frame.

Despite the ease of operation of concealed cup hinges, butt hinges are a traditional favorite for inset doors and are a less obtrusive alternative in glass-paneled cabinets, where the hinge is always in view.

7

TRIMMING TOP & BOTTOM

1 How a cabinet meets the ceiling—or doesn't—and how it meets the floor significantly affect a kitchen's looks. Here, upper cabinets are topped by a dropped soffit, which extends over the sink and counterspace, while base cabinets are finished off with a narrow toespace.

2 A double soffit makes the transition between a high ceiling and standard-height cabinets. The lower soffit is flush with the cabinet face, and the built-out soffit incorporates recessed lighting.

3 Frameless cabinets with glass doors meet a lowered soffit in this new Shingle-style house in Rhode Island.

4 In a beach-house kitchen, frameless cabinets stop short of ceiling joists to make a spot for odds and ends; the ledge takes off solo around the corner and above the staircase.

1 Beams and latticework shelter the kitchen space in this Prairie-style farmhouse. Beams align with 6-ft. 10-in.-high trim that runs throughout the house, and the latticework carries light fixtures.

2 Glossy-green European-style cabinets offer an extra-tall toespace. The soffit built flush over the wall cabinets adds a clean-looking detail.

3 Rather than stop short of the ceiling to make way for continuous open storage, these cabinets support niches that display decorative pottery.

4 Quartersawn red-oak cabinets stop short of the 8-ft. 8-in. ceiling to allow for a painted woodland frieze in this Arts and Crafts kitchen.

5 Cherry wall cabinets are hung from the ceiling and trimmed with crown molding.

TRIMMING CABINET TOPS

Stop wall cabinets at the standard height of 7 ft. and trim the top with a board cornice or other trim. Add light strips to showcase decorative kitchenware.

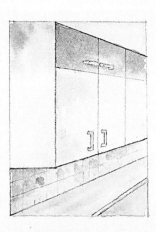

Take wall cabinets to the ceiling. Trim the joint or leave a narrow reveal, as shown here.

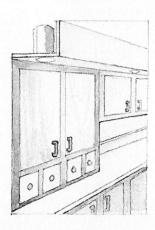

Build out the soffit over standard-height cabinets and use the plenum for lighting and ductwork.

Keep the soffit flush with the cabinets and trim the area with crown molding and half-round trim. Use the plenum for ductwork.

6

TOPPING OFF THE WALL CABINET

Wall cabinets are ideal for storing dishware, condiments, nonperishable food items, and any manner of things that small children shouldn't reach. Often, wall cabinets don't reach to an 8-ft. ceiling, partly because tall cabinets cost more, and partly because items stored up high are hard to reach. Open cabinet tops are ideal for decorative pottery or baskets, little-used kitchen tools, plants,

a painted frieze, or windows—natural light that enters a room at a high window provides the most desirable light year-round, and it bounces off the ceiling to multiply the effect.

Cabinets can also meet a lowered drywall or wood-trimmed soffit that often contains lighting and ductwork. For a more traditional look, cover a flush-fitting

lowered soffit with a super-deep crown molding to tie the cabinetry visually to the ceiling. If household members are prone to allergy or asthma, consider taking the cabinets to the ceiling or to a lowered soffit to avoid surfaces that collect dust.

Cabinets that reach the ceiling or a soffit often require trimming to hide the joint. An elaborate

molding can make the cabinet look more like furniture. Another option is to make a narrow slot—or a *reveal* in designspeak—between the cabinet and the soffit or ceiling. Storage at high altitudes is hard to reach, so consider making separate doors at the top of a tall wall cabinet for seasonal and seldom-used kitchen gear.

6 Stop cabinets short of the ceiling, take them all the way, or finish them off with a soffit. These drawings show just four of the many ways to trim the tops of cabinets.

1 Flat-brushed aluminum trim ties the tops of these cabinets together.

2 Traditional-style cabinets in a renovated farmhouse have no toespace, and the upper cabinets extend all the way to the ceiling.

3 As an accent to quartersawn white-oak cabinets, the toe-space and backsplash are trimmed with anodized aluminum strips. Cabinets are finished with a furniture wax/sealer and car wax.

4 The flat-paneled cabinets in this contemporary, open-ceilinged kitchen stop at a conventional 7 ft.; their tops provide gallery space for large decorative pieces.

1 These traditional cabinets have no toe-spaces—except at the dishwasher. But to make it comfortable to stand at the sink, the cabinet below the sink is recessed a few inches and the apron is canted outward.

2 Modeled after English unfitted cabinets, these Douglas fir cabinets take on the look of furniture, with legs that drop to the floor at the ends of cabinet runs.

3 To make good use of light and space in a small kitchen, cabinets on side walls stretch up to provide more storage, but cabinets on the window wall stay low. A tall window between the cabinets lets in as much light as possible, and a valance/ shelf holds dishware and contains recessed lighting.

TRIMMING CABINET BOTTOMS

This is a typical toespace at front with a flat cabinet side and shoe molding on each side.

Extra-tall European toespace trim board usually covers adjustable cabinet legs.

The toespace trim is continued along flat side with trim board.

Cabinet frame continues to the floor to become a leg.

The toespace is on the front and side; the side can be paneled to match the front.

This traditional cabinet has no toespace; base trim is optional.

Corner pilaster provides a leg for the cabinet; the curved cabinet bottom disguises the toespace.

Where a toespace is not provided, consider recessing the lower cabinet at the sink by 3 in. or 4 in.

4 A curved Douglas fir cabinet base makes a seamless connection with a concrete floor that is subdivided by wide strips of wood.

5 Fitting for a 200-year-old farmhouse kitchen, new cabinetry was designed with legs at the end of each case with an open toespace between (a dark-painted panel set 4 in. from the face acts as a backstop). Bright paint colors keep the kitchen warm even in winter.

THE TOESPACE NEEDS ATTENTION, TOO

The toespace (also called a toekick) is made by a separate, recessed platform that supports the cabinet. American-made face-frame cabinets and most frameless cabinets have a 4-in.-high, 3-in.-deep toespace. European cabinets often have tall toespaces—from 5 in. to 9 in. high—to cover the adjustable legs that are standard features in cabinets that are built to be movable. A tall toespace means less interior cabinet space, unless the toespace itself can be designed for storing platters, a pull-out skid or ladder, or other flat items.

A continuous recessed toespace would have been nonexistent in a residential 19th-century kitchen. It isn't that people were built differently back then, it's just that they worked at tables, and there's plenty of space between table legs. If you prefer traditional-style cabinets, you have several options for finishing the cabinet bottoms (see the drawings above). For example, drop the door sides to the floor and leave an opening between the resulting "legs." If curves are in your bag of style tricks, radius the corners of the opening between the stiles as if the cabinet were an individual piece of furniture.

But consider adding a dark-painted panel 3 in. or 4 in. back from the face of the cabinet; otherwise, the space under the cabinet will be a magnet for dust, errant garlic cloves, and other kitchen detritus. Or do without a toespace and increase the countertop overhang to 4 in. from the usual 1½ in. You'll want full-extension drawer guides if you pull out the countertops this far.

Toespaces can provide space for heat/air registers and ductwork to a central system, or even for installation of individual toespace heaters. The blowers in toespace heaters can be noisy, so research the options.

The toespace also acts as a bumper against overzealous mopping and vacuuming. If you opt for no toespace, consider adding at least a 4-in.-tall base trim to your cabinet. This detail can also apply to the sides of a cabinet, where it's not common to have a toespace. Here, a base trim provides a natural paint break or a change of material that allows for easier repairs if the bottom of the cabinet is damaged by man or beast.

6 The way a cabinet meets the floor affects its character (whether traditional or contemporary), how long the cabinet lasts, and how easy it is to work at the countertop. Cabinets can run straight to the floor without a toespace and may be trimmed or not. If there's no toespace, the countertop should have an overhang of 3 in. to 4 in. to make it easier to stand at the counter.

A PALETTE OF MATERIALS

1 Extra-wide stiles and rails with a square-edged bead give these cabinet doors unusual and pleasing proportions, further accentuated by the tall toespaces.

2 The faux finish on these cabinets looks like quartersawn oak, and the stile and rails are grained to look like ebony.

3 Stock cabinets can offer a surprising range of features, such as these tiny Shaker-style maple drawers with brushed-nickel pulls. Such narrow drawers don't require slides for stability.

4 Kitchen cabinets in a desert house are veneered with red plastic laminate, and the doors have top-to-bottom slabs of textured glass let into grooves at the edges. Handles are applied to the top corners of the glass. All countertops are butcher block. This kitchen has no upper cabinets because the view is just too good to miss.

Cabinets don't come in just a few colors anymore. There is hardly a finish, color, or material imaginable that hasn't appeared on or in a modern kitchen cabinet. Currently, maple is the most popular wood used in new cabinets, with oak and cherry tying for second place. Plastic laminate, a recent front-runner in kitchen-cabinet construction, is now the material of choice in about 10% of new kitchens; use of stainless steel is relatively uncommon but growing.

Wood may be the most popular look for kitchen-cabinet doors, but solid wood is only a small component of a cabinet, if it contains any solid wood at all. Solid wood can be used for drawer faces and doors, but wood-veneered (or plastic-laminated) plywood, medium-density fiberboard (MDF), and particleboard are common as well. New on the market is MDF shaped into a raised-panel design, with the entire door or drawer face finished with a PVC coating and paint.

WHAT'S IN A CABINET CASE?

You won't find solid wood in most of today's cabinet cases, except for the face-frame portion of a face-frame cabinet, and that isn't always solid stock. What you will find is that the sides, bottoms, and tops of a case—whether face frame or frameless—are built from sheet goods, also called sheet stock or panel products. Sheet goods are manufactured from wood, wood by-products, and even non-wood sources. The most common are plywood, MDF, and particleboard. All of these materials make cases that are significantly more dimensionally stable than solid wood.

Hardwood plywood is stronger and more water resistant than other panel products, but it also costs more. Many cabinetmakers are satisfied with MDF or particle-

board for budgets that don't allow for plywood. In fact, many factory-made cabinet cases are made of particleboard because it is dimensionally stable and provides a smooth face for plastic laminate and wood veneer. If your cabinets are made of particleboard or MDF, make sure that cabinet-case tops, bottoms, and sides are ⅝ in. or ¾ in. thick; anything less and the cabinet won't hold up for long. Thinner MDF or particleboard—¼ in. is typical—is fine for cabinet backs that don't require strength. MDF and particleboard like water about as much as the Wicked Witch of the West, so be sure all edges and surfaces are well covered with laminate or paint.

The exposed and semi-exposed surfaces (those that

are visible when the door or drawer is opened) of a cabinet case must be finished in some way, usually with a wood veneer or a laminate.

Wood veneers are available in many species; maple is common for the interior of custom-quality carcases. Laminates include vinyl and paper films, melamine, and high-pressure plastic laminate, which is the most durable. Thermofused melamine on particleboard won't hold up as well on doors or drawers, but it makes an ideal interior surface of a cabinet case. It is half the price of hardwood plywood, is washable and tough, cheaper than high-pressure laminate, and won't peel—unlike films and foils, which are not water-resistant.

1 Arts and Crafts–style cabinets are oak; its strong, dark character made it the wood of choice at the turn of the century. Alternating upper cabinets are paneled with leaded vision glass. A white tile backsplash and stainless steel brighten the dark oak and black-granite countertop.

2 Pine is historically accurate for Colonial-style cabinets; these are handplaned and have a hand-applied varnish finish.

3 A study was enlarged and turned over to kitchen space in this Spanish-style house, making room for simple and elegant cherry cabinetry.

ABOUT WOOD

Oak has always been a traditional favorite for cabinet doors and drawers because of its pronounced grain and flecks of color, especially abundant in quartersawn oak, which is more expensive but also more dimensionally stable. Recently, maple and other light, warm-colored wood species and stains have become more popular, and cherry is an elegant choice that naturally darkens over time. Pine is softer, with a comfortable, farmhouse-kitchen look.

Certain wood species are appropriate for certain historical styles. Quartersawn oak is a natural for Arts and Crafts-style kitchens, and Douglas fir was also common in turn-of-the-century cabinetry. Pine and maple were Colonial favorites, and either cherry or pine would be suitable for Shaker–style cabinets. For an antique look, apply finishes by hand.

Drawer fronts and doors of higher-cost cabinets are commonly made from solid wood, but solid wood is prone to shrinking and swelling with seasonal changes, so all edges require finishing. Cabinetmakers can allow for joints to move by building frame-and-panel doors, but gaps will show in painted cabinets when the frames and panels expand and contract at different rates. Cabinetmakers will not guarantee otherwise; that's the nature of wood. As a rule, hardwoods tend to age more gracefully than softwoods, which may crack and are softer and wider grained. However, applying wood veneer to plywood or MDF makes it possible to use practically any type of wood veneer and makes for a more dimensionally stable door or drawer than solid wood.

It's best to have wood cabinets finished in the factory or shop. This minimizes shrinking and swelling of the wood when it moves from shop to residence, allows better control of the finish, and allows for the use of finishes that can't be applied safely in a residence without adequate ventilation. Cabinets that are to be painted on site should at least be primed before delivery. Stain and paint colors appear in kitchen-cabinet brochures, but you will get a more accurate view if you look at actual stains on real cabinet doors before making a selection. Take a sample outdoors to view it in natural light. Be sure that the stain and the species match those you specify because each species takes stain a different way.

4 These unusual cabinets in a Texas kitchen have doors and drawers inset into frameless cases that have been edge-banded in mesquite. Wall-cabinet doors are sandblasted.

White is the most common color for new cabinets today, but it typically isn't the only color in the kitchen; dark wood, stainless-steel or black appliances, and open shelves full of colorful kitchenware add contrast. Mixing painted or stained surfaces with natural wood is part of the unfitted kitchen aesthetic, and it looks refreshing and homey. Cabinets can be painted and distressed to look old or even painted with faux graining. Only solid wood and wood-veneered plywood or medium-density fiberboard (MDF) can be stained or finished clear. MDF and particleboard are always painted (though occasionally an MDF door or drawer is given a clear finish) or finished with a factory-applied opaque coating.

1 A variety of finishes and colors enlivens a farmhouse kitchen.

2 Distressed cabinets frame a deep sink in this country kitchen.

3 Natural red-birch cabinets have the warmth of cherry but will not darken over time.

4 Hickory cabinets brighten up a traditional-style kitchen. The plate rack topping off the cabinets is real, but look closely and you'll see that the plates are painted on.

2 The cabinets in a new Shingle-style house on the Atlantic Coast were distressed and then stained red and blue.

1 The straight grain of Douglas fir contributes to the simple, serene look of turn-of-the-century-style cabinets. As in historic kitchens, these cabinets have no toespace.

3 Custom-made stainless-steel doors are fitted to manufactured frameless stainless-steel cases. Brushed stainless-steel wire pulls provide texture. The backsplash and countertop are black African granite.

4 These cabinet doors in a Manhattan loft were completely resurfaced with exotic bubinga, also called African rosewood.

Anyone with health or environmental concerns about the materials that go into making cabinets can check into the increasing number of "green" or environmentally gentle products being offered. Formaldehyde-free products such as hardboard from waste wood, particleboard from wheat straw, MDF from recycled paper, and wood veneers are becoming available for residential use. Check For More Information on pp. 196-197 for a guide to green building products.

5 This cherry face-frame island cabinet was distressed on the job site. The painted cabinets in the background are birch plywood with solid maple frames, doors, and drawer faces.

What's Inside?: Cabinet Accessories

1 It's often easier to find what you want in drawers or roll-out shelves than in cabinets with shelves. These drawers are wide, with D-shaped handles to make them accessible.

2 A slide-out shelf for cleaning supplies, swing-out shelves for canned produce, and full-extension drawers for pots and small appliances are just three of the accessory options available for base cabinets.

Although not as noticeable as other elements of the cabinet, accessories play a big role in how well a kitchen works. The best accessories--from appliance garages to lazy Susans—will suit a cook's work methods, storage needs, and budget. Cabinet accessories worth special consideration include slide-out and pull-out shelves, vertical slots for trays and baking sheets, good-sized spice drawers, and small-item racks that fit on the inside of cabinet doors. And most households would benefit from cabinet accessories geared toward recycling, such as pull-out twin trash receptacles and under-cabinet bins for compost.

3 This small kitchen for a retired couple is packed with extras. Appliance garages fit into leftover space at the corners of wall-oven cabinetry (far right), and a shallow storage cabinet beneath a counter is just wide enough for canned goods (right). A pass-through window overlooks a patio to the right (below).

1 The trapezoidal door panels of these sophisticated frameless cabinets open to reveal shelves in the upper cabinet and a slide-out drawer below. The drawer is custom-fit with graduated shelves.

2 A drawer with a stepped insert is a handy space for storing spices (left), while, for a cookie-cutter devotee, drawer dividers keep a collection sorted by size (right).

3 A new 3-ft.-wide skylit bay in this kitchen created space for a new sink with granite surround and a butcher-block countertop over Douglas fir base cabinets (left). Cutouts in the butcher block allow for easy disposal of vegetable trimmings, which drop to a compost bucket. Accessible only from the outside (below), the compost bucket is a short walk from the compost heap.

4 A slide-out cutting board just below countertop height provides an extra work surface in a kitchen tight on space.

1 Cabinets in an Arts and Crafts kitchen are chockfull of accessories for a serious cook, including a spice drawer; bread drawer; under-the-counter wine rack; tray-storage cabinet with vertical dividers; and two appliance garages housing swing-up shelves for a food processor and mixer, plugged in and ready to go with accessories on pull-out shelves below.

2 An urban kitchen benefits from the extra counterspace afforded by a pull-out serving drawer. The window opens onto an outdoor eating space.

3 An appliance garage keeps the clutter of coffee-making gear out of sight yet accessible.

If there's an empty corner inside your cabinets, chances are there's an accessory to fill it. Accessories can be fixed, such as an appliance garage or a narrow spice shelf under a wall cabinet, or they can be movable, such as a full-height, pull-out pantry or a lazy Susan. Hard-to-access corner cabinets can be fitted with a lazy Susan, pull-out drawers, half-moon swing-out drawers, or with an all-metal storage rack. A rule of thumb for cabinet accessories is that moving parts and full-extension accessories cost more. The multilevel, multipart, swing-out metal rack costs the most, and the simple, revolving lazy Susan costs the least. But the full-access ease of the corner rack may work better for your kitchen. The lowest-tech solution would be to keep the corner cabinet open and use it to store a trash bin on wheels that you can roll wherever you need it. Clearly, how you use your kitchen will determine which accessories you need. Here's what's available:

Storing recyclables and trash
This is a growing need in most kitchens. There are pull-out garbage and recycling bins, slide-out trays for trash cans, revolving bin containers, old-fashioned slant-top bins for recycled goods, under-counter composting buckets, and more. Keep in mind that you'll likely need at least two bins, one for trash and one for recycled goods, and try not to locate the trash bin under the sink, especially if yours is a two-cook kitchen.

Finding extra work space
Find extra counterspace in pull-out boards, pull-out tables, and swing-down surfaces. A cutting board that hooks over the countertop edge can be a handy fixture for heavy-duty kneading or chopping.

Pots and pans
For easy access, pots and pans can be out in the open on a pot rack or shelves or stored in extra-deep drawers or pull-out shelves next to the range. Drawers and racks are available just for storing pot lids, which get in the way when you stack pots and pans.

Drawer trays
If all you've ever known is the tangled-utensil drawer, take a look at the multitude of tray inserts in plastic or wood. Inserts can separate cutlery or peelers from pizza wheels. If you prefer utensil storage at countertop height, look for racks that fit at backsplash height. Often-used silverware—the real stuff—will benefit from a drawer insert that is fitted with silver cloth to minimize tarnish.

Storing dishware
Wood dish racks are back in vogue, and most cabinet manufacturers offer them. Glassware can be stored on stemware racks built inside or under wall cabinets.

Storing appliances
The popular small-appliance storage accessory is the appliance garage, which usually is built in under a cabinet and has a tambour or swing-in door. Appliance garages work best if you don't "park" other items in front of them. Mixers and processors can be stored on heavy-duty swing-up shelves.

Storing knives
Consider safety when storing knives. Blades shouldn't be a hazard to children or adults. Specify built-in slots in the back of a countertop or store knives in a swing-down rack. Magnetic strips are available for knife storage, or drawers can be ordered with knife-slot inserts built in.

Storing flat items
Baking sheets, cutting boards, and trays can find a custom-made home inside your cabinets with little problem. Cabinetmakers can build tray slots into cabinets and leave them open or cover them with a door. The toespace is an ideal spot for a pull-out drawer for holding baking sheets and roasting pans. Consider storing long, narrow items in a vertical-slot cabinet above the refrigerator.

Storing food
Cabinet accessories are available for storing any kind of room-temperature food: canisters for flour, sugar, beans, coffee; tiered shelves for storing cans; pull-out wire drawers for potatoes and onions (don't store them in the same bin—they aren't compatible chemically); back-of-cabinet racks; and multi-row, multilayered, full-height swinging pantries. The space shuttle couldn't ask for more.

Storing breads
Crusty breads get flabby and stale in the refrigerator; freezer or room-temperature storage are better options. A stainless-steel bread box with ventilation is available for countertop, under-counter, or in-drawer locations.

Storing spices
Spice drawers have several rows of angled trays set into the drawer. Spices may have to be kept in same-size jars, and not all spice-company jars will fit, so check sizes first. A spice drawer next to the cooktop may be handy but won't be beneficial to long-term spice storage. A cooler spot is better. Narrow spice shelves or wire spice racks can often handle a variety of spice bottles; again, keep spice racks away from the range except for basic, often-used spices, such as salt, pepper, and red-pepper flakes.

Storing cleaning supplies
Pull-out racks for cleaning supplies are handy under the sink or next to it. There are hooks, trays, and racks for any number of cleaning supplies. A popular item in kitchen-cabinet showrooms is the pull-down sink front for storing sponges and brushes. But will you really keep a damp sponge here and retrieve it every time you need to use it? It's not really that practical, although it is handy when company comes and the workhorse sponge needs hiding.

Storing dish towels
Dish towels can be stored for daily use on pull-out towel rods that recess into a slot or on a rack inside a cabinet door. Long cabinet pulls are ideal for storing dish towels (they'll dry faster, too), or towels can be stored on pegs on a cabinet side.

4 A lazy Susan under a cooktop makes maximum use of an otherwise wasted space.

5 Roll-out drawers behind quartersawn oak doors have full-extension side-mount slides that are rated for heavy loads.

SHELVES AND PANTRIES

Cabinets have traditionally been the repositories for all manner of kitchen goods, from small appliances to food to dishes. But two trusty old-kitchen elements have been rediscovered that bring both food and gear to the forefront. The first is the much overlooked open shelf. Studies in a test kitchen at Cornell University in the 1950s concluded that narrow, open shelves from the countertop to head height provide easiest-to-reach storage. It's taken a long time for the wisdom of the Cornell study to catch on in modern kitchens, although kitchens from centuries past often had no other means of storage. There's also something comforting about shelving. Shelves are alcoves that both shelter and show off our possessions, whether dishes, books, or spices. We all admire well-organized workshops or studios stacked with raw materials and tools, displayed not only for ready access but also because the materials and the tools are beautiful in themselves. Where better to display the tools and materials of the trade than in the kitchen, a workshop if ever there was one?

Not everything in a kitchen needs to be on view or immediately at hand, however. Enter the second old-kitchen feature, the pantry. The word *pantry* finds its origins in a French term for bread store. The bread storeroom of yore held not only bread but also table-ware, linen, and candles, all overseen by—what else?—the pantler. Pantlers aren't likely to be for hire today, but fully half of new kitchens include pantries. These new pantries store ready-to-eat foods, such as dry cereal and crackers, and quick-to-fix foods, such as soups and pasta. They also make room for pet food, paper goods, and recycling containers.

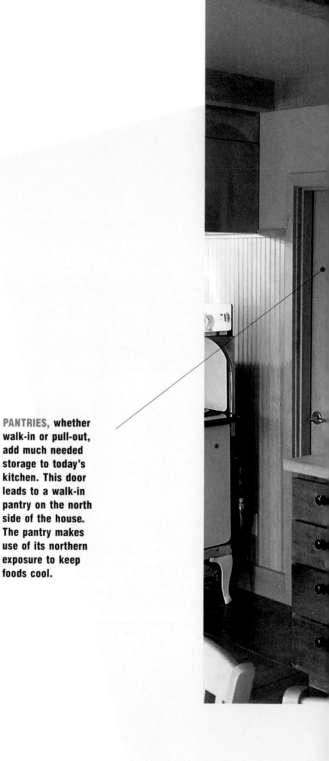

PANTRIES, whether walk-in or pull-out, add much needed storage to today's kitchen. This door leads to a walk-in pantry on the north side of the house. The pantry makes use of its northern exposure to keep foods cool.

OPEN SHELVES supplement cabinet storage and make it easier to reach frequently used items. Here, open shelving requires only a one-step motion for taking down dishes to serve to the table and a one-step motion to unpack them from the dishwasher.

SHELF SUPPORTS can be visible, such as metal or ornate wooden brackets, or invisible, such as the shelf pins that hold up these shelves. The whole unit is supported by the wall and cabinet below.

SHELVES display bulky items without the need for expensive cabinet space. This top shelf shows off a collection of baskets and one-of-a-kind kitchenware.

THE OPEN SHELF

1 Small openings and long openings balance out in this whimsical shelf unit. Crown molding above the shelf is echoed in the backsplash molding, which widens to become a narrow shelf at right.

2 The otherwise wasted space under the stairs provides shelf room for an assortment of dishware and spices.

3 A timber-framed barn-turned-summer house on Martha's Vineyard can afford to have its stud space filled with shelving rather than insulation. More wares are on display in island shelves.

A shelf can go anywhere—in a 5-in. recess along the length of an island, in the space between a wall cabinet and the window, or in the awkward space under a stair. Or shelves can be grouped as a deliberate wallful, such as in a bookcase or china cabinet. Let shelves overlap their casework to make sills if that's appropriate. A shelf can also be long, such as one that spans the window over the sink or a plate rail running throughout the breakfast nook, or it can be a mere few inches for holding one decorative piece. Shelves can be movable or built in.

1 Minimal shelves supplement closed storage in a house for one person. Custom-built metal and wood shelves carry the kitchen gear and a long, cantilevered wood-slab shelf holds dishes.

2 An oak-veneered grid of shelves buffers the kitchen from this stair hall and becomes the gallery for the family's collection of Japanese artifacts.

3 Not all dishware and cooking gear is consigned to closed cabinets. Here, a continuous 8-in.-deep shelf runs above the countertop along both sides of the kitchen and carries decorative objects, appliances, and baking staples.

4 In a San Francisco house, deep-set shelves are recessed into the plaster walls. The effect is of vernacular masonry walls in houses along the Mediterranean.

5 A shallow shelf big enough for one layer of bottles, books, and odds and ends is built into the back of a large kitchen island.

6 A two-shelf plate rack brings a splash of color to a simple country kitchen. The countertop is Carrera marble.

1 It isn't exactly a shelf, but this steam-bent white ash dish rack takes the place of one, and allows for air-drying at the same time.

2 These dishware shelves are suspended from a wood frame affixed to the ceiling, keeping them within reach but out of the line of sight between cook and diners.

4 This mountain-side kitchen turns its pantry inside out to display everyday food items next to antique tins in the spirit of a general store.

3 Graduated-depth shelves make it easier to work at the countertop. Here, a 12-in.-deep shelf is 30 in. above the countertop (the standard at sinks and cooktops). Lower shelves become shallower as they get nearer the counter. Consider what spices, oils, tools, and dishes to store at hand and size open shelves accordingly.

GRADUATED-DEPTH SHELVES

Upper shelves are full 12-in. depth (same as standard wall cabinets).

A 12-in.-deep shelf at 20 in. to 30 in. above the counter is a good place for task lighting.

Lower shelves are stepped narrower for ease of working at the counter.

Open shelving not only makes it easier to grab a pot, wooden spoon, or plate but also makes it easier to put away these items after cleanup. Shelving spreads out storage rather than stacking it in a harder-to-reach cabinet. Utility isn't the only force behind the rebirth of open shelving. Looks count for a lot. Open shelving provides visual interest in a kitchen and makes a nice counterpoint to yards of closed cabinetry.

1 In an energy-efficient house, the kitchen is separated from the sunspace by three sections of a segmented glazed garage door. To increase the light to the kitchen, shelves are thick, bevel-edged lengths of glass supported on plywood brackets.

2 Prerusted steel support angles extend past the cabinets to carry glass shelves. A steel plate is accordioned to hold wine.

3 In a house with only windows from waist-height up, a simple, ceiling-hung plywood shelf with plastic-laminate surfaces provides a spot for oversized pots.

4 Mahogany-backed niches display individual Arts and Crafts ceramics. A continuous plug mold below the wall cabinets allows appliances to be used practically anywhere in the kitchen.

5 The shelving is designed like compartments in an old roll-top desk. The shelves are supported in dadoes (slots) in the upright boards to give the shelf unit clean, finely crafted detailing.

A LOOK AT SHELF MATERIALS AND SUPPORTS

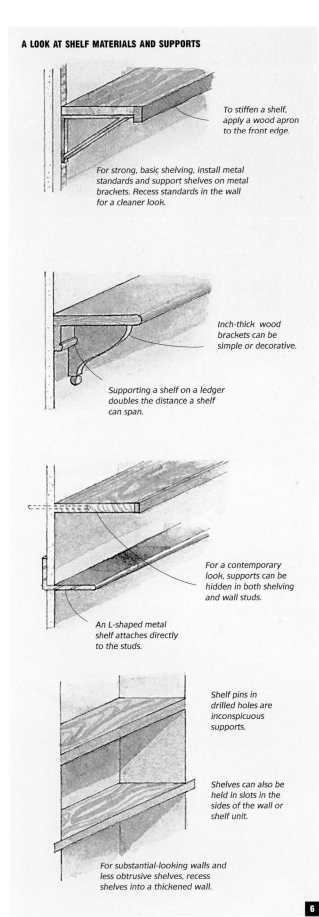

To stiffen a shelf, apply a wood apron to the front edge.

For strong, basic shelving, install metal standards and support shelves on metal brackets. Recess standards in the wall for a cleaner look.

Inch-thick wood brackets can be simple or decorative.

Supporting a shelf on a ledger doubles the distance a shelf can span.

For a contemporary look, supports can be hidden in both shelving and wall studs.

An L-shaped metal shelf attaches directly to the studs.

Shelf pins in drilled holes are inconspicuous supports.

Shelves can also be held in slots in the sides of the wall or shelf unit.

For substantial-looking walls and less obtrusive shelves, recess shelves into a thickened wall.

6

7 Skinny shelves for trays and platters are topped off by a stepped niche that displays a graduated set of ceramic kitties.

8 Much of the kitchenware in this renovated 200-year-old house is stored on restaurant-grade Metro shelving, which aligns with the new wide-board cedar wainscoting. The 1x10 pine floor was painted with a checkerboard pattern.

6 Shelves can be made of solid wood, hardwood plywood, particleboard, medium-density fiberboard, glass, or metal. All shelves require support. They can rest on metal or wood brackets, on invisible shelf pins, or be recessed into the wall.

8

THE PANTRY REDISCOVERED

1 A pine-paneled pantry with a roofing-slate countertop provides storage for dishware and serving pieces and makes a pleasant secondary workspace.

2 In a Federal-style townhouse, pantry storage shares the below-grade entry hallway with storage for coats, cleaning equipment, and other gear, all disguised behind elegant, raised-panel doors. The kitchen is just out of sight to the left.

3 This kitchen pantry packs a lot of goods into a free-standing storage unit, shelves supported by standards, and back-of-door shelf units. A plate rail above the door molding provides display space for Arts and Crafts pottery.

There's no doubt that the pantry is in the midst of a major revival. But after years of being kept out of new kitchen plans, why the flurry of interest in the pantry? We no longer store barrelsful of flour, cornmeal, and sugar in the pantry, nor do we put up preserves for the winter that often. Baking staples still find their way into pantries, but in 5-lb. bags of flour or a can or two of baking powder. What's filling up the rest of the modern pantry is a prodigious quantity of prepared foods or quick-to-prepare foods. Where else to put 25 shapes of pasta, each family member's favorite cereal, and the range of dog food from dry to moist? Bulk-buying of nonperishable items at discount warehouses adds more to the shelves, too. Another function of the new pantry is to handle recycling containers, which are rightfully taking up more space in kitchen plans.

1 The pantries in these plans all add convenient storage space in or near the kitchens they serve; some help out with additional space or facilities. Inside pantries, look for laundries, a second sink, access to the cellar, an additional freezer. Several pantries make up for storage that would otherwise be in wall cabinets so that walls can be given over to windows or shelves.

A pantry and laundry room combined

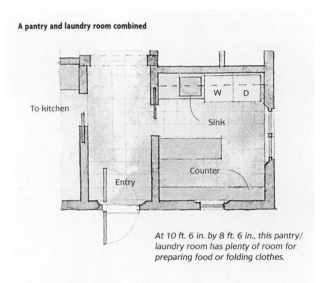

To kitchen

W   D

Sink

Entry

Counter

At 10 ft. 6 in. by 8 ft. 6 in., this pantry/ laundry room has plenty of room for preparing food or folding clothes.

An open pantry within arm's reach

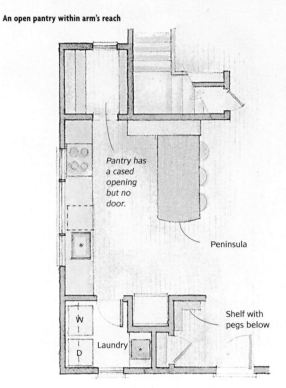

Pantry has a cased opening but no door.

Peninsula

Shelf with pegs below

W
D

Laundry

A pantry instead of wall cabinets

In a kitchen with a great view and no upper wall cabinets, a 5-ft.-square pantry and open shelves make up for lost storage.

Pantry

Kitchen

Under-counter refrigerator

1

2

2 An in-kitchen pantry packs canned and dry foods in narrow shelves built into the doors. Baskets organize small items that might otherwise get lost.

3 In a 1930s-style kitchen, pantry contents are partly obscured by a scrim of brass mesh secured by red-lacquered trim.

3

A pantry in the 19th and early 20th centuries meant either a food-storage pantry (also called a cold room, cold store, or store room) or a butler's pantry. The butler's pantry (or dish closet) stood between dining room and kitchen and contained cupboards for dishes, drawers for linens, and, ideally, a sink. Present-day pantries don't have to be walk-in. Pantries can be squeezed into corners or alongside cellar steps. Entire pantry cabinets are available from cabinet manufacturers, including swing-out or slide-out units with narrow shelves top to bottom.

4 A butler's pantry in the corner of the house allows for far-off views through a little window just above countertop height.

5 Careful planning and special hardware make maximum use of this pantry with its built-in door shelves and swing out storage. Bottles, cans, and packages are held in place by a short lip.

1 This pantry is built on the north side of a house in Wyoming; it buffers the kitchen from cold but takes advantage of the chill to keep foods cool. A sink and countertop (behind the door) provide space for food and drink preparation.

EGGS IN THE PANTRY?

In Europe, a pantry for storing fresh foodstuff is called a larder. Americans may find it startling to see photos of a European larder, where vegetables, lemons, eggs, cheese, and butter (and, rarely now, lard) are stored. Larders are ideally cool, dark, and well ventilated, but are they capable of storing dairy products and vegetables—other than root and bulb vegetables? It's argued that Europeans shop frequently and use the food in the larder quickly, but North Americans are discouraged from letting eggs *in the shell* sit out for even three hours and are admonished to keep cheese, lemons, butter, and broccoli in the refrigerator.

This concern about spoilage and the fact that we are buying both more fresh produce and more frozen prepared main dishes than ever are the reasons we increasingly use the *refrigerator* as a pantry, or larder. The difficulties with storing all fresh foods and dairy products in the refrigerator are that many fruits suffer from the too-cold depths of the refrigerator, most cheeses must be brought to room temperature before they taste good, and refrigerators, therefore, are getting fatter. A happy medium is to store borderline items, such as fruits, in a cool pantry in the cellar or along a north wall and leave the dairy products in the refrigerator. Just don't forget to take out the Stilton at least an hour before dessert.

2 Face-frame cabinets in the dining room look elegant when closed (above left) but contain a pull-out pantry that can pack an amazing amount of food and kitchen supplies into a narrow but deep space (above right).

3 An existing butler's pantry received an Arts and Crafts makeover to match the rest of the house. The countertop is African mahogany and the backsplash is granite; wall cabinet doors contain leaded-glass panels.

COUNTERTOPS AND BACKSPLASHES

Cabinets may be the packhorses of the kitchen, but countertops are the workhorses. That's where we lay out supplies, peel and chop, roll and knead, mix and serve. It's fair to say that the countertop is like the carpenter's workbench. It needs to be tough, level, smooth, and big enough for the work we do. A kitchen needs at least one 36-in. continuous countertop space, preferably sinkside. For two cooks, provide two separate 3-ft. counters. Refrigerators and cooktops require landing spaces on one or two sides. Any hardworking kitchen will demand even more countertop space but locate it outside the work triangle (between refrigerator, sink, and cooktop) to keep meal preparation efficient.

A countertop—and its vertical helpmate, the backsplash—bestow a kitchen with much of its style. Both can be highly polished, satin, or matte, and their edges can be profiled in several ways. A variety of materials serve well as countertops, from ages-old wood and marble to the heatproof, waterproof choice of the restaurant-kitchen, stainless steel. Always economical, plastic laminate comes in an ever-widening array of colors and patterns, as does the more expensive but longer-lived solid-surface countertop. Richly colorful, formable, and durable, concrete is coming into its own as a countertop material. A backsplash can be more decorative than a countertop, because it serves not as a work surface but as a protective one. Here's where three dimensions can come into play, such as in a bas-relief tile panel or a backsplash-turned-shelf. Finally, there's no reason why a kitchen can't be fit up with more than one type of countertop material, each customized to suit the task.

A BACKSPLASH BEHIND A COOKTOP is essential. A stainless-steel backsplash not only protects the wall from spattering food, but it also angles out to make a narrow shelf for spices and whatnots.

COUNTERTOPS in food-prep workspaces should be durable and moisture resistant. This concrete countertop can also handle hot pots.

CONCRETE can make a subtly colorful countertop surface. In this sophisticated city kitchen, the concrete has a soft, green tint; while the sculptural divider has a matte finish, the hard-working concrete countertops are ground to a polish.

RAISING A COUNTER to elbow height makes it comfortable for a standup drink and chat with the cook. This tapered and curved concrete divider is cast-in-place concrete.

BACKSPLASHES AND COUNTERTOPS keep spills away from cabinets and walls. Here, stainless steel takes shape as an all-in-one backsplash, integral sink, and countertop—all thoroughly waterproof.

A SURFACE FOR EVERY TASK

1 A stainless-steel countertop makes a high-tech counterpoint to wood cabinets. The countertop level drops at right, and granite takes over to make a pastry counter.

2 The primary countertop on this freestanding kitchen breakfront is granite; a lower-height butcher-block table provides a surface for chopping fruits and vegetables.

As in our grandparents' day, countertops today aren't necessarily of all the same material, nor are they always the standard 36 in. high. It can be practical—and stylish—to mix and match countertop materials and heights to suit different kitchen tasks.

If plastic laminate, the most economical of countertop materials, covers most of a kitchen's counters, there might be money left over to spend on a granite countertop around the range. Stainless-steel countertops over base cabinets and a wood surface for the kitchen table/workspace are a good working duo. The contrast of cool and warm colors and hard and soft textures suits both form and function in all styles of kitchens.

3 White plastic laminate need not be plain Jane. Here, it adds light to existing cabinets that were painted with oil-base eucalyptus and lavender. A new backsplash of Indian slate tile adds another level of texture and color. To the left of the range is a wood chopping block.

4 A cutting board that fits tightly over a sink extends the working surface of a tile countertop. The board has a cutout so vegetable trimmings can be swept into the sink and garbage disposal below.

1 Concrete and wood meet on a countertop in a house in the Pacific Northwest. The cantilevered wood cutting boards slide onto the concrete to make a surface for chopping vegetables or serving a snack.

COMFORTABLE COUNTERTOP HEIGHTS

2 Countertops are usually set at 36 in., but that's not always the optimum height. Here are comfortable countertop heights for various kitchen tasks.

A 42-in.-high countertop works well for sitting, eating, and some kitchen tasks.

Cooks may find it easier to wash dishes at a 38-in. to 40-in. counter, especially if the sink is deep.

A 36-in.-high countertop handles most kitchen tasks and suits the average-height cook. Taller cooks may prefer 38-in. or higher counters.

Kneading bread and rolling out pastry are best performed on a lower surface, from 29 in. to 31 in. above the floor.

Countertops can overhang cabinets, or their nosings can be flush with the surface of the cabinet. Today, countertops often have a mere ³/₄-in. nosing overhanging the cabinet. This detail makes for a trim, elegant look, but it does call for diligence in cleaning up spills before they ooze over the edge of the countertop. The countertop overhang protects the cabinet below to a certain extent. It's been known for veneered cabinets with a flush countertop nosing to delaminate due to liberal use of the sink sprayer (not uncommon in households with small children). If spills are a real concern, avoid the flush look and go for a 1¹/₂-in. overhang.

If toespaces aren't historically correct in your kitchen or if you just don't like toespaces, a deep countertop overhang of 3 in. to 4 in. will make it much easier to work at the counter.

3 Three countertop surfaces handle different tasks. A butcher-block counter covers the food-prep island, solid surface covers the base cabinets and handles most countertop tasks, and tiles inset into the counter next to the range provide a landing spot for hot pots and pans.

4 In a new Art Deco–style kitchen addition, four countertop surfaces see plenty of action. The low marble counter is used for baking tasks, while sink countertops are stainless steel. Slate takes over next to the restaurant-style range, and in another part of the kitchen there's a butcher-block insert for chopping vegetables. Tile covers all workspace wall surfaces.

PLASTIC LAMINATE & SOLID SURFACE

1 For economy, good looks, and watertightness, black plastic-laminate countertops are fabricated with an integral backsplash. Because the laminate is dark, the square nosing shows no dark seam.

PLASTIC LAMINATE

Since its invention in the 1910s, plastic laminate has come to dominate the residential kitchen-counter market. Manufactured by many companies in hundreds of colors and patterns, it is the least expensive countertop material available today. Plastic laminate is easy to install, wipes clean easily, and has good stain resistance. On the downside, it isn't impervious to stains, it can't be cut on, and it scorches easily. A surface wound can't be easily repaired, and seams are visible, but unobtrusive if done well. Although plastic laminate itself resists water, if water gets into a seam, it can damage the particleboard substrate. Sink cutouts in plastic-laminate countertops should be sealed thoroughly, and it's also important to seal the joint between sink and countertop so that no water can get through.

A square edge (called a self edge) of a light-colored plastic-laminate countertop exposes the dark line of its kraft-paper core. This can be left as a design feature, or it can be covered by metal or wood trim. A fairly new alternative is to attach a beveled piece of matching or contrasting plastic-laminate trim. Where a drop-in appliance fits, the countertop must be finished with a squared edge, not a beveled edge, or there will be a dirt-collecting valley between the appliance and the countertop. Another alternative is to select a dark color, so the dark line doesn't show.

Solid-core laminate has a through-the-body color, so it shows no dark line. Its drawbacks are a higher cost, fewer colors and patterns, and a reputation for being brittle.

2 Plastic laminate with a wood nosing is the primary countertop material in a small kitchen for two. A lowered, butcher-block countertop faces the breakfast bar and living area.

3 Solid-surface countertops can be fabricated with integral solid-surface sinks, as in this Hawaiian kitchen. Solid surface is also fairly resistant to heat, and light scorch marks can be sanded out.

PLASTIC-LAMINATE NOSINGS AND BACKSPLASHES

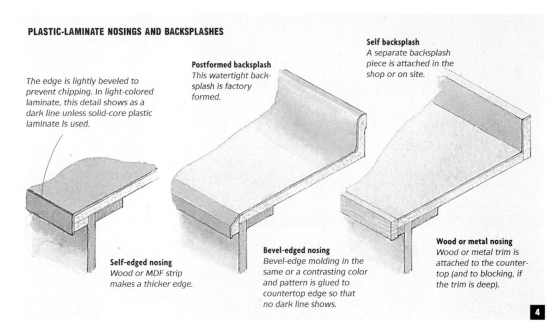

The edge is lightly beveled to prevent chipping. In light-colored laminate, this detail shows as a dark line unless solid-core plastic laminate is used.

Postformed backsplash
This watertight back-splash is factory formed.

Self backsplash
A separate backsplash piece is attached in the shop or on site.

Self-edged nosing
Wood or MDF strip makes a thicker edge.

Bevel-edged nosing
Bevel-edge molding in the same or a contrasting color and pattern is glued to countertop edge so that no dark line shows.

Wood or metal nosing
Wood or metal trim is attached to the counter-top (and to blocking, if the trim is deep).

4 Plastic-laminate countertops can be finished with a square edge (known as a self edge) or a bevel edge or with a strip of wood or metal. The backsplash can be formed as an integral part of the countertop or added as a sepa-rate piece.

5 Three solid-surface countertops have three different nosings. At far left, the countertop is fin-ished with a contrast-ing nosing with a classically profiled top edge. The white countertop at left received a beveled top edge, while the stone-like countertop at right was given slightly eased top and bottom edges.

1 A gray solid-surface countertop with a stone-like pattern makes a handsome countertop in a California house. The backsplash behind the cooktop is stainless steel.

2 To allow heat to dissipate quickly, solid-surface countertops are installed without a solid substrate. Nosing and backsplash options are shown below.

3 Contrasting solid-surface colors can be joined without a visible seam. The purplish-blue square in the backsplash is echoed in a smaller version in the contrasting nosing.

SOLID-SURFACE NOSINGS AND BACKSPLASHES

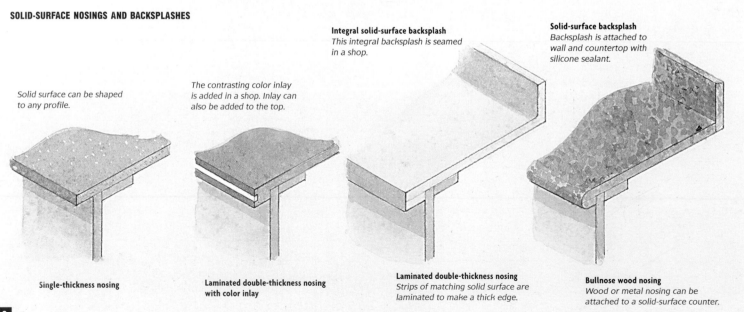

Solid surface can be shaped to any profile.

The contrasting color inlay is added in a shop. Inlay can also be added to the top.

Integral solid-surface backsplash
This integral backsplash is seamed in a shop.

Solid-surface backsplash
Backsplash is attached to wall and countertop with silicone sealant.

Single-thickness nosing

Laminated double-thickness nosing with color inlay

Laminated double-thickness nosing
Strips of matching solid surface are laminated to make a thick edge.

Bullnose wood nosing
Wood or metal nosing can be attached to a solid-surface counter.

ABOUT SOLID SURFACE

Solid surface has been around only about 25 years, but it has claimed almost one-third of the residential countertop market. This material is basically a plastic, but unlike plastic laminate it is homogenous, so scratches and stains can be sanded or ground out and polished if necessary. Solid-surface countertops are waterproof, even at the seams, and for the ultimate waterproof detail, a solid-surface sink can be integrated into the countertop. As a rule, seams are invisible, but not all patterns follow this rule.

Solid surface comes ½ in. or ¾ in. thick for countertops and thinner for backsplashes. For a more substantial edge, add a strip of the same-color solid-surface material to make a 1-in. to 1½-in. edge. The material is almost as dense as stone but fairly workable—in fact, it can take just about any nosing profile—but only manufacturer-certified craftspeople can install it.

So what are the drawbacks to this miracle material? Namely, it's expensive—twice the price of the most expensive laminates and the same as lower-priced granite. But its healing benefits, its resistance to heat and water, and its large palette of colors and patterns make it a popular and long-lived choice.

4 In sync with the early modern range, this retro red plastic-laminate countertop is finished with a ribbed metal nosing. White plastic-laminate cabinets open with touch latches.

5 The center of this kitchen table is a mottled-gray plastic laminate; the edges are finished with a wood-grain laminate. Here, the exposed dark brown of the laminate core is used as a design feature.

6 Beige plastic laminate gets a facelift from a thick wood nosing and cobalt-blue backsplash. The backsplash cap becomes both spice shelf and windowsill.

WOOD

1 In a townhouse kitchen, face-grain wood countertops received several coats of nontoxic polyurethane to resist moisture from the stainless-steel sink and spills from the cooktop. A backsplash with flat-profiled rectangular white tile recalls kitchens of the 1920s and 1930s.

2 Edge-grain butcher block is the material of choice in the kitchen of a desert house, while plastic laminate takes over for cabinet doors.

ABOUT WOOD

Wood can work beautifully as a countertop if it is properly maintained and finished. Butcher block is the most common wood product for a working countertop; it is usually made of 1½-in. maple strips laminated together with edge grain up. Traditional end-grain butcher block is porous, so it is considered unsanitary for use in restaurant kitchens, and face grain is far too soft for a cutting surface. But wood with the face grain up (meaning that the boards are wider than butcher block) makes a handsome serving or eating counter—just don't cut on it.

Wood can be sealed with a nontoxic polyurethane (under-sides sealed, too, to prevent warpage), and any wood countertop around a sink requires several coats on all exposed surfaces. A wood countertop used for chopping fruits and vegetables (meats only on portable, washable cutting boards, please) can be left unsealed and maintained with periodic rubdowns with mineral, tung, linseed, or other nontoxic oil (but not vegetable oil, which turns rancid).

Wood is the easiest to work of all countertop materials and can take many nosing profiles. It costs twice the price of plastic laminate but only one-third the price of granite.

3 A large island with a butcher-block countertop, cooktop, and food-prep sink is the centerpiece of an inviting kitchen in the San Juan Islands, Washington.

4 A poplar countertop is edged with an irregular 2-in.-thick strip of cypress to make a weighty and singular surface.

5 Wood countertops are traditionally butcher block, but flat wood boards and removable wood cutting boards are workable options.

WOOD COUNTERTOPS

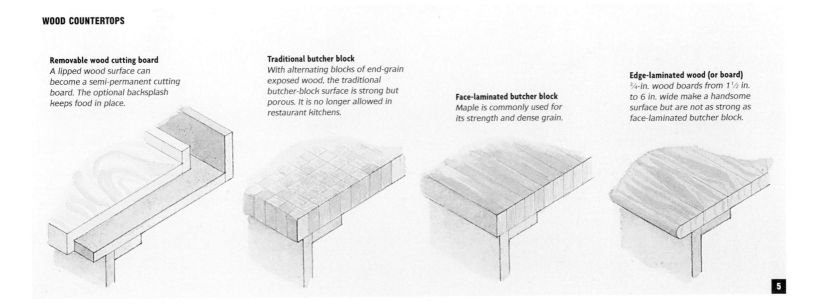

Removable wood cutting board
A lipped wood surface can become a semi-permanent cutting board. The optional backsplash keeps food in place.

Traditional butcher block
With alternating blocks of end-grain exposed wood, the traditional butcher-block surface is strong but porous. It is no longer allowed in restaurant kitchens.

Face-laminated butcher block
Maple is commonly used for its strength and dense grain.

Edge-laminated wood (or board)
3/4-in. wood boards from 1 1/2 in. to 6 in. wide make a handsome surface but are not as strong as face-laminated butcher block.

STAINLESS STEEL

1 Stainless steel is artfully shaped into an integral sink, backsplash, and countertop in this city kitchen. The nosing has a lipped, or marine, edge to contain drips. The concrete countertop divider is tinted a light green, and the plaster walls are soft yellow.

2 Stainless steel can be shaped to form its own nosing and backsplash.

STAINLESS-STEEL COUNTERTOPS

For a sturdy countertop choose 16 ga. or thicker steel (the smaller the gauge number, the thicker the steel). A plywood substrate helps muffle noise.

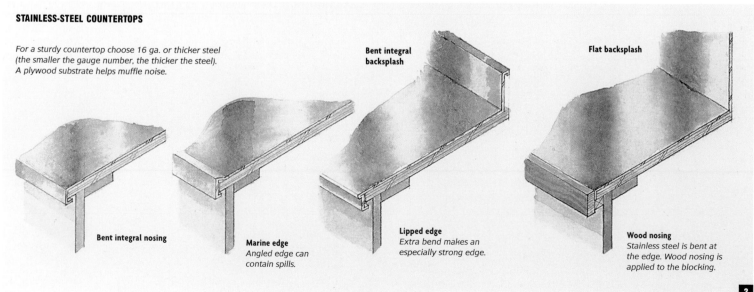

Bent integral nosing

Marine edge
Angled edge can contain spills.

Bent integral backsplash

Lipped edge
Extra bend makes an especially strong edge.

Flat backsplash

Wood nosing
Stainless steel is bent at the edge. Wood nosing is applied to the blocking.

3 This full-height brushed-stainless-steel backsplash deflects water and provides a softly reflective surface between the matte solid-surface counter-top and the highly reflective cabinets.

ABOUT STAINLESS STEEL

For the ultimate in watertight-ness and heat resistance, stainless steel is the answer. It can be shaped and seamed to provide its own nosing, backsplash, and sink, and it is extremely long-lasting; a prefabricated stainless-steel sink can be welded into the countertop to save money. Stain-less steel is also very easy to clean—another reason it's the mainstay of the restaurant kitchen—and it makes a good surface for rolling out pastry.

The strongest stainless-steel countertops are 16 ga. to 14 ga. (the lower the number, the thicker the steel). Stainless-steel coun-tertops should be set on ¾-in. plywood for added strength and to dull the sound.

Stainless steel compares to solid surface in price, so it's fair-ly expensive. It also scratches easily, but that's not usually an aesthetic problem because the scratches give the countertop a satin look. Some think stainless steel is strictly modern, but it can look historically correct, at least for kitchens emulating 1930s or 1940s kitchens, which often had dull silver-colored counter-tops made of monel, which is one-third copper and two-thirds nickel.

4 Stainless-steel receptacle plates fit precisely into this ele-gant, carefully crafted stainless-steel coun-tertop and back-splash. The counter-top at left is con-crete, tinted a soft shade of green. The range hood is a cus-tom design.

TILE

1 Stone tile makes a durable and handsome pattern for a backsplash. Countertops are granite, thinner over base cabinets and thicker where the counter covers a wide island.

2 This tile kitchen countertop looks like a fish market, with lifelike crabs and fish; a couple of bas-relief crabs are escaping.

ABOUT TILE

Tile's greatest asset is its looks. It can take on practically any shape, any color, and any size and can add spice to a dull kitchen even in small amounts. If you require the smoothest of counters for baking or food preparation, count on using boards to work on because tile isn't uniformly smooth. It does make a great surface for serving because of its superior heat resistance and good looks.

For best protection against water and stains, choose a glazed, impermeable tile. Such tiles can be glossy or matte. If you lean toward the ultra-matte look of unglazed ceramic or stone tile, confine it to a backsplash that isn't behind the cooktop or sink. Tile countertops look beautiful, and they are extremely durable, heat-resistant, and long-lived. Tile itself is resistant to scratching, and if it weren't for the grout, it would be highly resistant to stain. Epoxy grout costs more than standard grout and is harder to work, but it is a good choice for tile countertops and backsplashes in the kitchen because of its hardness and superior resistance to staining and mildew.

Tile can be finished off with a wood or metal edge, or it can have a self edge at the nosing, meaning that it is edged with specially shaped tile. One nosing has a gentle no-drip edge called a V-cap.

3 Ceramic tiles from the Netherlands make an elegant backsplash for a solid-surface countertop. Fitting the uneven, hand-molded tiles to the uneven post of a 200-year-old house was a challenge well met.

4 The rust, lavender, and soft-green colors found throughout the kitchen come together in this luminous three-dimensional tile backsplash.

5 A riot of vegetables and fruit makes a bright backsplash over a polished-stone countertop.

2 Ceramic tiles from a resurrected 19th-century pottery company make the perfect backsplash in an Arts and Crafts kitchen remodel. The counter and lower backsplash are granite; the backsplash trim cap is oak.

1 A double-height backsplash of granite and crackled-glaze tile makes an effective and handsome finish under the wood apron of the window.

3 Four tiles that match the backsplash tiles are inset into the solid-surface countertop next to the range. Although solid-surface can take some heat, tile can take more.

4 Hand-painted tile is combined with commercially available tile for a backsplash that's both decorative and economical.

5 A hand-painted tile mural makes a gorgeous backsplash for a pair of sinks. Surrounding the mural and making up the rest of the backsplash are commercially available tiles.

6 This tile countertop is made up of 8-in.-square tiles that are edged with a thick oak nosing to match the cabinets.

TILE COUNTERTOPS

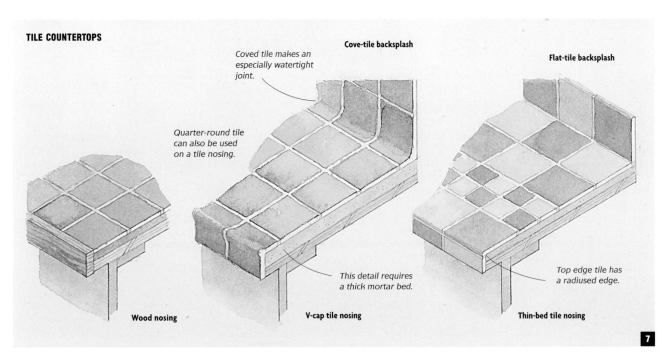

Coved tile makes an especially watertight joint.

Cove-tile backsplash

Flat-tile backsplash

Quarter-round tile can also be used on a tile nosing.

This detail requires a thick mortar bed.

Top edge tile has a radiused edge.

Wood nosing

V-cap tile nosing

Thin-bed tile nosing

7 Tile countertops can be finished off with a tile nosing (in various styles) or with wood. Backsplashes are coved or flat.

STONE

2 For a heatproof surface with wood in the details, this granite countertop is trimmed with a Douglas fir nosing.

1 When it isn't mealtime, the granite-topped island is used for baking and food preparation. Countertops, backsplash, and sink are Vermont soapstone. Beadboard fills in as a wall covering above the backsplash.

3 Wood brackets support a cantilevered countertop of ³/₄-in.-thick granite in this California kitchen.

4 Roofing slate turned upside down makes a good-looking and durable stone tile countertop.

Granite and marble are the most common stones used on kitchen counters, but slate and soapstone are coming into their own, and limestone can make a beautiful countertop if it is carefully sealed. Granite is, above all, hard. It's also the least porous of the stones, although it can be damaged by alcohol, and it's easily cleaned with warm water and a mild neutral cleaner, such as detergent.

Marble is softer and, because it is somewhat porous, it will stain, especially if exposed to acidic foods. But it is wonderfully smooth and cool and works well as an inset countertop for pastry making. Some bakers prefer a portable marble countertop—a smaller, say, 20-in.-square, piece of marble that they can chill in the refrigerator before making pastry. Such a piece of marble needs cushioned pads on each bottom corner to

keep it from scratching the countertop below.

Stone slabs are usually $^3/_4$ in. or $1^1/_4$ in. thick. The thinner width slab should be applied over a plywood or other rigid substrate, but a thicker stone slab can support itself. Any stone requires support from a bracket, brace, or supplemental substrate if it overhangs its support by more than 12 in. To make a $^3/_4$-in. slab look thicker, have a $^3/_4$-in. strip of the same stone affixed to the edge and finish the edge as one piece. Both granite and marble can be highly polished or honed to a satin finish. All stone should be sealed with a penetrating sealer, which lasts for years.

Selecting granite or marble can be daunting, but don't rely on a small sample for how your countertop will look. Visit the stone yard to

view cut slabs up close. Some designers and contractors require their clients to sign off on the slab after seeing it in person. But check again when the granite or marble is dressed and finished and arriving on site. Be sure to talk with the designer or contractor about seams: where they go and how the stones will look when joined.

Stone (especially granite) can be the most expensive countertop material of them all, but prices vary widely depending on where the stone is quarried and dressed and how it is finished. For an economical use of stone, confine to select locations, such as near the cooktop, as a lowered pastry-making surface, or as a serving countertop. Check a stone yard for small, less-expensive pieces.

5 The nosing of this $1^1/_4$-in.-thick Vermont verde marble countertop has a Dupont profile. This type of marble is as hard as many types of granite.

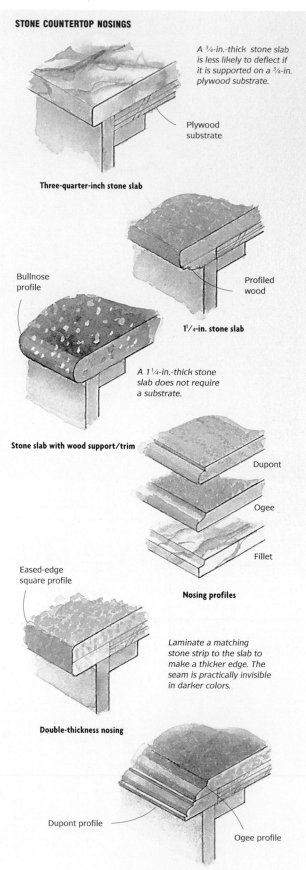

STONE COUNTERTOP NOSINGS

A ¾-in.-thick stone slab is less likely to deflect if it is supported on a ¾-in. plywood substrate.

Plywood substrate

Three-quarter-inch stone slab

Profiled wood

Bullnose profile

1¼-in. stone slab

A 1¼-in.-thick stone slab does not require a substrate.

Stone slab with wood support/trim

1 A bullnosed granite countertop sits atop oak cabinets with home-grown mesquite handles in a Texas kitchen.

2 Indian slate tiles make a dramatic wall-high backsplash behind a cooktop and stainless-steel countertop.

3 Stone nosings can be profiled in a number of ways. The most common profiles are shown in the drawing.

Dupont

Ogee

Fillet

Nosing profiles

Eased-edge square profile

Laminate a matching stone strip to the slab to make a thicker edge. The seam is practically invisible in darker colors.

Double-thickness nosing

Dupont profile

Ogee profile

Double-thickness nosing with two different profiles

4 A green-tile backsplash continues up the wall to make a handsome frame for the window over the sink. The counter-top is peach-colored marble.

5 A 2-in.-thick slab of marble is low enough to make a handy surface for preparing food or eating lunch. There's a striped butcher block around the sink, and black slate makes up cabinet backsplashes and countertop.

CONCRETE

1 In a kitchen without cabinet toe-spaces, a countertop that cantilevers 4 in. provides space for a cook's feet. This cast-in-place concrete countertop has a chamfered 2-in. lip. The concrete was ground to make this rich, variegated texture, and several coats of sealer have kept it easy to clean and resistant to stain.

2 Countertops and the 8-in.-deep shelf behind them are covered with Fireslate, a portland-cement-based material that looks like slate. Although it is sealed, Fireslate is somewhat porous and acquires a warm, variegated patina with use.

ABOUT CONCRETE

Concrete makes a tough, beautiful countertop material that is resistant to scratches and heat, and it can cost less than a same-size countertop in solid surface, stainless steel, stone, and most tile. Concrete is either cast in place or precast. Today concrete can take on a wide range of colors and textures, which can be through the body or added to the surface after the concrete is placed or after it has cured.

3 This L-shaped concrete countertop was cast in two pieces and then joined with connectors and epoxy and sealed with a tough, moisture-cured urethane. A 4-in. band of $^3/_8$-in.-thick weathered and sealed copper makes a novel backsplash.

4 This West Coast kitchen features concrete countertops and backsplashes. Look closely at the cooktop backsplash and you'll see that family members have left their mark with handprints in the concrete.

5 A salvaged Creole cottage has a concrete countertop cast first with regular bag-mix concrete and then with $^1/_2$-in. topping concrete, which levels itself. High windows provide privacy; tall backsplashes are wood.

6 Cast-in-place concrete countertops can be finished with a square or bevel edge. Bevel edges are formed by placing triangular strips in the formwork. Square edges are more difficult to cast cleanly.

CAST-IN-PLACE CONCRETE COUNTERTOPS

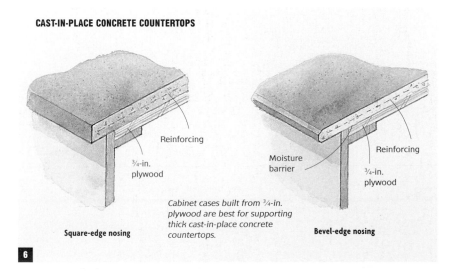

Reinforcing

$^3/_4$-in. plywood

Moisture barrier

Reinforcing

$^3/_4$-in. plywood

Cabinet cases built from $^3/_4$-in. plywood are best for supporting thick cast-in-place concrete countertops.

Square-edge nosing

Bevel-edge nosing

1 These concrete countertops are in the same kitchen. Both are at least 3 in. thick and are tinted, one with black and the other with blue. The sink countertop intersects with an untinted concrete support. The penetrating sealer used to finish the concrete can't prevent staining, so a rich patina develops over the years.

2 This simple square-edged countertop was given a subtle curve at the seating area. While it looks like concrete, this countertop is, in fact, zinc.

3 An ocher concrete countertop with an elaborate nosing is paired with Moorish-influenced tile to make a handsome and durable workspace.

ABOUT FIRESLATE

Fireslate, a proprietary product, appears in the concrete section because, like concrete, it is primarily a portland cement product. But Fireslate is always cast by the manufacturer. It started life as a laboratory countertop and hearthstone because it resists direct heat of up to 500°F.

It's fairly easy to work using masonry cutting and shaping tools. Fireslate needs sealing before it can repel water and grease, and even then it can't help but gain a rich, mottled patina over time. Scratches are easy to sand out with steel wool.

4 Lower counters and backsplashes are Fireslate, which is heat resistant. The upper serving counter is cherry, and the integral sink and surround are stainless steel.

5 This island has a 1½-in.-thick concrete counter, while the base cabinets are topped with black granite. Concrete and granite must each be sealed before use, but concrete develops a rich patina over the years.

APPLIANCES AND SINKS

Appliances and sinks make the kitchen what it is, a space for storing, preparing, and cooking food. Consider style, kitchen layout, cooking and eating habits, and energy efficiency when selecting these kitchen basics. Before making a visit to a big appliance store, with its endless rows of appliances, get a running start by winnowing out appliance sizes and configurations that won't work for your kitchen, and then focus on the details you consider important. For example, side-by-side refrigerators offer certain pros and cons; refrigerators with top or bottom freezers have others. Once the size and configuration are chosen, look at shelf options, drawer possibilities, freezer details. Likewise, cooking gear can be broken down into configurations. Do you prefer a range, which consolidates cooking functions and heat, or will a separate cooktop and oven suit your larger, multi-cook kitchen?

In the case of sinks, configuration and material choice go hand in hand. Certain materials work best in certain shapes and sizes. Choose a sink configuration once you know where the sink will go, by how dishes are washed (by hand, dishwasher, or both), and by whether or not there's space, plumbing, and money for a second sink. Faucet details and sink accessories come next.

It may help to look at the appliances and sinks in these kitchens from several points of view. First look at style, then take a look at how the individual elements work. Finally, observe how appliances and sinks work in relation to each other and to the rest of the kitchen elements.

POT RACKS over an island can hold everyday cooking gear as well as out-of-the-ordinary kitchen accessories, such as the oversized teapot and blue glass rolling pin shown here.

REFRIGERATORS can be built-in or freestanding, depending on design preference and budget. This built-in stainless-steel refrigerator has a side freezer as well as three bottom drawers. On the left is an ice drawer and on the right, two crisper drawers.

TWO SINKS (here, one on the island and the other on the main run of countertop) are a great asset for the multi-cook kitchen. Make sure there's space for a countertop drainboard and drain, even if 99% of the dishes go in the dishwasher. The dishwasher here is to the left of the main sink.

VENTILATION HOODS—not just an open window or a recirculating fan—are essential in kitchens that contain professional-style cooking gear.

COOKING GEAR options include cooktops, ovens, and, as shown here, professional-style ranges.

COLD STORAGE: REFRIGERATORS

A refrigerator with a freezer on top is the most common model, even though a refrigerator door gets opened many times more than the freezer. A bottom-freezer refrigerator is easier on the back (and on the toes if a container of frozen soup slips). Nevertheless top-freezer models are cheaper to buy. Both bottom- and top-freezer models are more energy efficient than side-by-side refrigerators. The virtues of a side-by-side model are that its doors are narrower and therefore don't swing out far, that it easily accommodates in-door ice and water dispensers (and optional water filters), and that it's more accessible to people with physical disabilities. Still, in addition to costing more to buy and run, many side-by-side models aren't wide enough on either side for party platters or big frozen pizzas.

1 Not everyone wants to hide the refrigerator. This ample model is at the outer edge of the work space to make it accessible to visiting family members. The space above is ideal for cookbook shelves.

2 A freestanding refrigerator can be surrounded with cabinetry to minimize its bulk and to make it look like its more expensive built-in cousin. Just be sure the doors can open fully and allow about 3/4-in. clearance around sides and top.

3 A built-in side-by-side refrigerator is finished with painted panels to match those in the rest of the kitchen. Along with stainless-steel microwave, wall oven, and sink, the refrigerator handles provide a bright contrast to the pale cabinetry.

4 Refrigerators come in a multitude of sizes. Here, 36-in.-wide refrigerators stand side-by-side to show differences in height, depth, and capacity. Built-in refrigerators are taller than freestanding models but not as deep. As a rule of thumb, side-by-side refrigerators have less capacity than top- or bottom-freezer models. They also have a larger proportion of freezer volume to refrigerator volume.

HOW REFRIGERATORS STACK UP

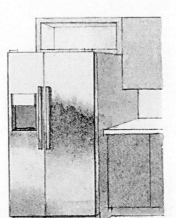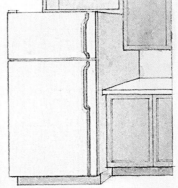

Built-in refrigerators
(36 in. wide, 24 in. deep, 84 in. tall)

Freestanding refrigerators
(36 in. wide, 30 in. deep, 66 in. tall)

	Side-by-side	Bottom freezer	Side-by-side	Top freezer (can be bottom freezer)
Refrigerator volume	12.5 cu. ft.	15.7 cu. ft.	15.2 cu. ft.	16 cu. ft.
Freezer volume	8.9 cu. ft.	6.4 cu. ft.	6.2 cu. ft.	7 cu. ft.
Total volume	21.4 cu. ft.	22.1 cu. ft.	21.4 cu. ft.	23 cu. ft.

Note: All side-by-side models have freezers on the left.

BUILT-IN OR FREESTANDING?

Refrigerators can be built-in or freestanding. The motor and coils that run a freestanding refrigerator are situated below and behind the food compartments, making it deeper than a built-in model, whose motor is either on top or on the bottom. The typical freestanding refrigerator measures from 27 in. to 32 in. deep, quite a bit deeper than the typical 24-in.-deep base cabinet. To reduce the apparent bulk of a freestanding model and to make it look built in, case around its sides and top, leaving enough room for doors to open and air to circulate. A more expensive detail is to pull out base cabinets flush with the refrigerator box (again, leave room for the door to open) and put a 30-in.- to 32-in.-deep countertop on the base cabinets. Panel the sides of the refrigerator for the most built-in effect. Or purchase one of the new 24-in.-deep freestanding models, which can be more easily cased to look built in.

At 2 ft. deep and 7 ft. tall, built-in refrigerators are shallower than freestanding models so they can align with standard cabinets; the shallow depth also makes it easier to see what's stored inside. Built-ins can be custom covered to match cabinetry or not (note that most stainless-steel panels have too low an iron content to hold refrigerator magnets; high-ferrous stainless-steel panels can be special ordered). Count on a built-in refrigerator to be about twice the price of a high-end freestanding refrigerator. A freestanding commercial refrigerator has a price tag that's even higher, and it also costs more to run than a residential refrigerator.

1 This refrigerator is built into a box that includes a broom closet at right, a food-storage pantry at left, and a stacked washer/dryer behind the pantry.

2 A refrigerator recessed into the wall is positioned just outside the work center to allow diners to access the refrigerator without stepping on the cook's toes.

3 A stainless-steel refrigerator brightens a richly colored Arts and Crafts–style kitchen.

4 These two separate freezer compartments are paneled to look like cabinet doors.

5 Separate refrigerator and freezer compartments are easily camouflaged. Without the door open, it would be hard to tell there's a refrigerator here at all. Drawers below can be freezer drawers, refrigerator drawers, or simply cabinet drawers.

WASHING UP:
SINKS AND DISHWASHERS

1 Big enough to handle stacks of dirty pans or an 8-qt. stockpot, this integral stainless-steel sink is a boon to both cooking and cleaning.

2 A slate sink and backsplash are beautifully integrated into Shaker-style cabinetry. Slate is heat-resistant and durable and is available in several colors.

3 This ceramic aproned farmhouse sink is mounted to the underside of a granite countertop. The wide-spread faucet is a reproduction model.

Stainless steel

Sinks made of stainless steel are relatively gentle to dropped dishes, come in many shapes and sizes, are easy to care for (go for brushed rather than shiny finishes), can handle hot pots, and don't seem to go out of style. The best sinks always have an 18% chromium content and a sound-dampening undercoating. Go for 20-gauge or, better, 18-gauge stainless steel (remember, a lower gauge number indicates thicker metal). Stainless-steel sinks are available as self-rimming, flush, or undermount.

Enameled cast iron

Sinks made of enameled cast iron (also called porcelain-enamel cast iron) are handsome and extremely durable. They come in many colors and are commonly self-rimming. Undermount sinks are also available but may need a support carriage. Because enameled cast iron is thick, the interior of the bowl won't be quite as big as a stainless-steel sink that could fit in the same space. Enameled cast-iron sinks are pricey compared to the average stainless-steel sink. Today's enamel isn't likely to chip, but it may not withstand a dropped cast-iron pan. A dropped wine glass, on the other hand, will itself shatter against an enameled cast-iron sink.

Enameled steel

Enameled-steel sinks are the least expensive, thinnest, and noisiest sinks and are easily chipped. Unless your budget is austere, don't buy one for a high-use area. Better styles have a plastic resin coating on the underside, which supports the enamel coating and softens the tinny sound.

Ceramic

Although similar to enameled cast-iron sinks in heft and hardness, ceramic sinks are not quite as resistant to chipping. A good-looking current model is the aproned farmhouse-style sink.

Solid surface

Solid-surface sinks are most often fabricated to be integral with a solid-surface countertop, making a seamless and watertight assembly. Such sinks must be fabricated and installed by trained and licensed craftspeople. Though expensive, solid-surface sinks are extremely durable, easy to clean, and homogenous, making it easier to repair the rare stain or chip.

Composites

Composite sinks haven't yet established long track records. They are molded from acrylic resins and crushed minerals, such as quartz. Available in more colors than solid surface, composite sinks can take more heat than solid-surface sinks but are also more likely to scratch (don't use abrasive cleanser).

German silver

German-silver sinks have a beautiful finish, have been known to last a century, and are exceedingly expensive. These reproductions of high-end butler's pantry sinks are made of nickel-silver, which is a malleable, corrosion-resistant alloy of copper, zinc, and nickel. There's a characteristic "S" curve between bowls for strength. Because the soft metal is kind to fragile dishes, German-silver sinks are recommended for washing china and glassware or for used as a potting sink for gardeners. Iron utensils and cookware will stain these sinks.

Slate and soapstone

Slate and soapstone (and occasionally granite) sinks are made of slabs that are fit into slots and glued together with watertight glue. For the biggest visual impact, they are usually fabricated with integral backsplashes and aprons and, often, flanking countertops. Stone sinks are expensive but you can specify practically any size and depth. They are highly heat-resistant (but always avoid setting a boiling hot pot on a freezing cold surface).

A sink is the most used piece of equipment in the kitchen. It's not an appliance (although it may contain a garbage disposal), but it is a workhorse nonetheless. The standard sink is traditionally 6 in. to 8 in. deep, but many homeowners prefer the new 10-in. to 12-in. sinks for handling big pots and lots of dishes. Deeper sinks keep water from splashing out, a benefit especially when a high-neck faucet is used. Taller people may find a deep sink uncomfortable because they have to bend over more; raising the countertop a few inches will make a deep sink easier to use. On the other hand, wheelchair users, or anyone who sits at the sink, will appreciate a lower countertop and/or a shallower sink.

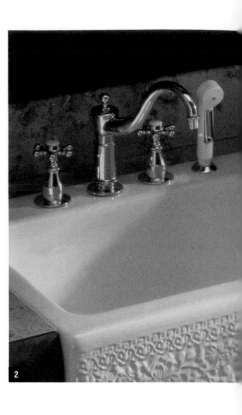

2 Considering how often we use our sinks, it's not surprising that all sorts of accessories have been dreamed up to make them handier, including soap dispensers, chilled-water spigots, and recycling chutes. Here, a handheld sprayer makes quick work of washing vegetables in a food-prep sink.

1 Maple countertops give way to teak around the cleanup sink in this rustic house. The round sink with gooseneck fitting (in the foreground) is right next to the range for filling pots.

A SURVEY OF SINKS

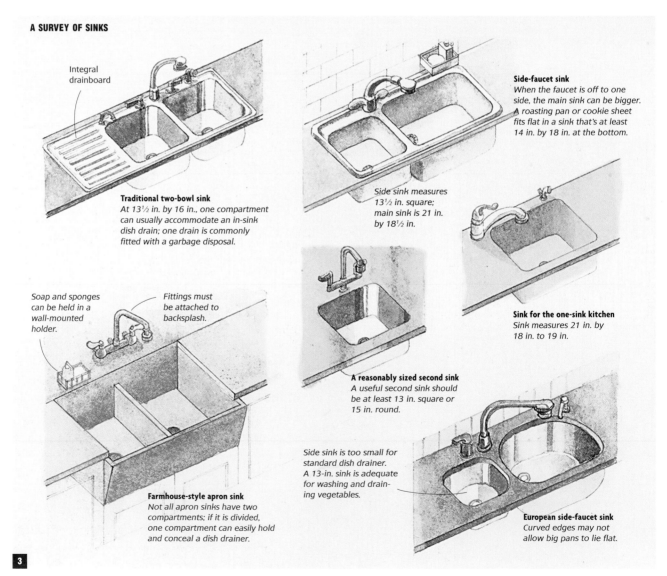

Integral drainboard

Traditional two-bowl sink
At 13½ in. by 16 in., one compartment can usually accommodate an in-sink dish drain; one drain is commonly fitted with a garbage disposal.

Side-faucet sink
When the faucet is off to one side, the main sink can be bigger. A roasting pan or cookie sheet fits flat in a sink that's at least 14 in. by 18 in. at the bottom.

Side sink measures 13½ in. square; main sink is 21 in. by 18½ in.

Soap and sponges can be held in a wall-mounted holder.

Fittings must be attached to backsplash.

Sink for the one-sink kitchen
Sink measures 21 in. by 18 in. to 19 in.

A reasonably sized second sink
A useful second sink should be at least 13 in. square or 15 in. round.

Farmhouse-style apron sink
Not all apron sinks have two compartments; if it is divided, one compartment can easily hold and conceal a dish drainer.

Side sink is too small for standard dish drainer. A 13-in. sink is adequate for washing and draining vegetables.

European side-faucet sink
Curved edges may not allow big pans to lie flat.

3 Sinks are available in one-bowl or two-bowl configurations and in varying sizes to suit different kitchen tasks.

4 An English-made faucet stands proud of the counter, making an elegant, easy-to-clean connection to the wood countertop. A rubber stopper on a chain in a porcelain undermount sink is a reminder of home for a U.S.-stationed family from England.

Choose a faucet when you choose a sink. A self-rimming sink will have holes drilled in its back ledge for a faucet, while the countertop behind an undermount sink is where faucet holes are cut. A faucet can be operated by separate hot and cold controls (called valves) that are either *center-set*, with valves and spout clustered over a single hole cut in countertop or sink ledge, or *wide-spread*, with valves set 4 in. or 8 in. apart.

Wide-spread faucets require three holes to be cut in the countertop or sink ledge. Single-control faucets require just one hole. Separate controls are more traditional, but single controls are easier to operate, especially with long, easy-to-move levers. Anyone who works with raw meat will appreciate a faucet that can be turned on with an elbow or the back of a hand. Farmhouse-style sinks with deep aprons and integral backsplashes usually require a wall-mounted faucet.

Then there's height. High-neck faucets look wonderful and are great for filling a tall pot and for swiveling between two large sinks. A high-neck spout also allows room to wash hands even if the sink is full of dishes. But keep in mind that water falling from a high-neck spout tends to splash out of a shallow sink. A sprayer, whether it retracts into the faucet or mounts on the sink or countertop, can fill tall pots, too, even when they're out of the sink (as all children know). Some spouts and sprayers can switch between full flow for filling pots and an aerated flow for rinsing.

It helps to know a little about how faucet valves work. Older faucets have valves with rubber compression washers that require periodic replacing, and some European companies still offer compression washers. But washerless faucets are the current standard, led by long-lived ceramic-disk valves, which use tightly fitted disks that slide across each other to open or close.

Underneath whatever fancy finish you like, the best faucet is made of noncorrosive solid brass (brass is made primarily of zinc and copper). Today's favorite finishes include chrome plating, nickel plating, and white enamel coating; also look for the new, nontarnishing brasslike finishes.

5 These two European-made faucets incorporate single levers and retractable sprayers, making them easy to use and requiring only one hole to be cut in the sink or countertop.

6 This commercial-style stainless-steel sink with two big bowls and an apron makes a fashionable contrast with traditional wood cabinets and divided-light windows in a California hill house.

1 Two good-sized bowls and a gooseneck faucet allow big pots to fit into the sink for filling and washing.

2 A food-prep sink facing the kitchen and dining room has abbreviated cabinet doors below to make it easier to stand at. On the other side of the wall are the scullery sink and dishwasher.

3 The way a sink fits into the countertop is determined both by the sink material and by the countertop material.

No matter how much you use a dishwasher, there will always be a need for a place to dry dishes and cookware. A second sink that is at least 14 in. square at the bottom can hold a standard rubberized-wire dish-drying rack. If a drying rack sits on the counter, it needs something to catch the water, whether it's a clean dishtowel, a removable rubber or plastic drainboard, or a drain that's integral with the countertop. Sinks can be fabricated with drainboards attached, or the countertop (if it's concrete, Fireslate, stone, or solid surface) can have drainage channels cut into or ridges affixed to the surface. A simple, flat 1/4-in. recess carved or cast into a countertop can keep water from spreading yet leave a countertop that's smooth and therefore handy for tasks other than draining dishes.

HOW SINKS FIT INTO COUNTERTOPS

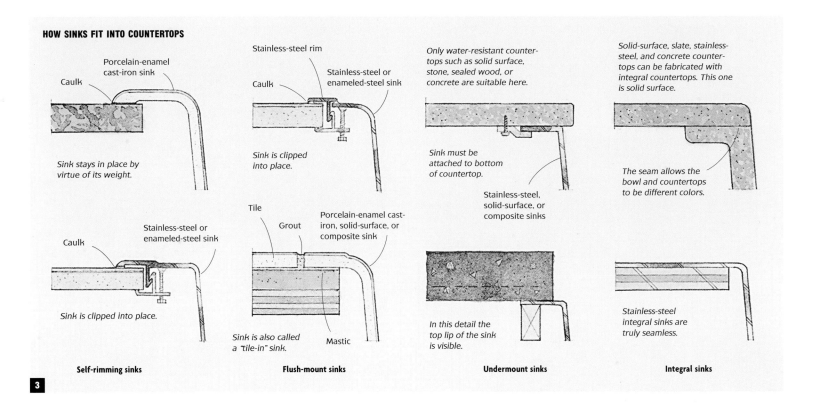

Caulk

Porcelain-enamel cast-iron sink

Sink stays in place by virtue of its weight.

Caulk

Stainless-steel or enameled-steel sink

Sink is clipped into place.

Self-rimming sinks

Stainless-steel rim

Caulk

Stainless-steel or enameled-steel sink

Sink is clipped into place.

Tile

Grout

Porcelain-enamel cast-iron, solid-surface, or composite sink

Sink is also called a "tile-in" sink.

Mastic

Flush-mount sinks

Only water-resistant counter-tops such as solid surface, stone, sealed wood, or concrete are suitable here.

Sink must be attached to bottom of countertop.

Stainless-steel, solid-surface, or composite sinks

In this detail the top lip of the sink is visible.

Undermount sinks

Solid-surface, slate, stainless-steel, and concrete counter-tops can be fabricated with integral countertops. This one is solid surface.

The seam allows the bowl and countertops to be different colors.

Stainless-steel integral sinks are truly seamless.

Integral sinks

3

4

4 This single-bowl undermount stainless-steel sink fits into a Fireslate countertop. The countertop was given a gentle slope to aid drainage.

5 This freestanding commercial sink, acquired second-hand, is 7 ft. long with a 12-in. back-splash. To minimize the sink's bulk, coun-tertops were designed to match the level of the backsplash.

5

COOKING GEAR

1 The big fireplaces in Colonial houses are inviting, but the back-breaking labor of cooking in them certainly isn't. In a new house built to look 200 years old, this fireplace is designed to be big enough to cook in, even if pop-corn and marshmal-lows are the primary fare. The window in the back of the fire-box is a historical detail.

2 A standard resi-dential slide-in range becomes a design feature when it is topped by a towering, burnished-steel range hood.

3 A separate cook-top is the best choice in this big, multi-cook kitchen. Locating it across from the sink makes it easier to fill pots and drain pasta and vegetables. A wise design detail was to raise the por-tion of the island meant for diners, which delineates the cooking area and keeps hot cookware away from diners.

COOKTOPS, OVENS, AND RANGES

4 Take a stroll through this cooking appliance store to savor the rich variety of cooking-gear options.

Double wall ovens
Ovens can be radiant (thermal), convection, microwave, or dual-duty.

Drop-in cooktop
Cooktops have a variety of heat sources; some units have interchangeable grills, griddles, and burners.

Single wall oven
Oven can be placed either under a drop-in cooktop or higher in a full-height cabinet.

Commercial-style cooktop
A stainless-steel apron overlaps cabinet case. This cooktop requires a hood vent.

Commercial-style range
Unlike a true commercial range, this unit is insulated and can abut walls and cabinets (oven doors still get hot). It requires a hood vent..

Commercial-style cooktops and ranges have up to eight burners or an assortment of burners, grills, griddles, and other options. Burners are hotter than standard (15,000 Btus compared to 7,000 Btus). Always provide adequate ventilation.

Drop-in range
Range rests on cabinet base.

Slide-in range
Sides are unfinished.

Freestanding range
Can fit between cabinets or be placed at end of cabinet.

4

Twenty years ago, most new kitchens featured 30-in.-wide, 24-in.-deep, freestanding, slide-in ranges with four burners and a single thermal oven. For the most part, that's still the case today. But as a rule, the just-above-basic new range will likely have a cooktop that's easier to clean, an oven that's self-cleaning, and time and temperature controls that provide more options.

Ranges aren't the only option today. Separate cooktops and ovens are taking up larger chunks of the kitchen budget. And there is a mind-boggling matrix of options for both ranges and separate cooktops and ovens (see the sidebars on the pages that follow).

5 A sculptural range hood provides a natural way to highlight the most important appliance in a cook's kitchen—the cooktop. This range hood is lined with stainless steel and finished with plaster on expanded-metal lath welded to an angle-iron frame.

5

1 Perfectly suited for the renovation of a small urban bank, a stainless-steel assembly of range, backsplash, and hood contrasts with traditional face-frame, no-toe-space cherry cabinets.

2 A drop-in range with a simple, downdraft vent is suitable for low-pan, moderate-heat cooking. A double-height stretch of tile makes a handsome and simple backsplash behind the cooktop.

3 A microwave built into a wall cabinet requires a deeper than usual cabinet. Cabinets tend to outlive microwave ovens, so make it easy to remove the oven without disassembling the cabinet.

4 There's a range hood hidden under the cabinets in this kitchen remodel of a 1950s Arizona desert house.

COOKTOP OPTIONS

Today's cooktop options include grills, woks, griddles, rotisseries, and dual-fuel combos. Before purchasing any equipment that requires more than a turn of a knob to operate, consider how much use it will *really* get and whether or not it requires special cookware and utensils; look to store the modules so they are easy to find and switch.

For folks who cook a lot but don't have a big budget, the best place to spend money is on good-sized burners spread far enough apart to handle four or more big pots and pans at once. Cooktops are available with porcelain-enameled steel, stainless-steel, or smooth ceramic-glass finishes. Look at edges, joints, and trim for ease of cleaning.

Gas cooktops provide instant heat that's easy to adjust and turn off, and you can always tell when a burner is on. In many parts of the country gas costs less to operate. The downside to gas is that it can be a source of indoor air pollution if ventilation isn't adequate. Today's gas burners run both cooler and hotter. One of the best inventions found in the gas cooktop is the sealed gas burner. This burner has no openings under the gas ring, so spills stay on the surface instead of drooling into a dark pit beneath the cooktop, and heat is more efficiently directed to the pot. An unsealed burner is usually rated 9,000 Btu (British thermal units), but it loses up to a quarter of that heat. Many mid-range sealed-burner cooktops offer a combination of burners, with low heat for simmering (about 5,000 Btu), high heat for sautéing (12,000 Btu), or medium heat (9,000 Btu)

for most tasks. Pricier professional-style ranges offer one or more burners rated 15,000 Btus, which is said to heat an 8-qt. pot of pasta water to boiling in 6 minutes, as well as intermittent-off burners that keep foods at a low simmer without scorching. Professional-style gas cooktops often have continuous grates, which make it easy to move a pot anywhere on the cooktop.

Standard electric cooktops are less expensive to buy than gas but more expensive to operate. A large electric-coil burner can actually heat a pot of water faster than a standard 9,000-Btu gas burner but it isn't as easy to control and takes a long time to cool. The old stand-by electric coil heats up and cools down faster than a disk-type electric burner. Electric disks or coils can be covered with a smooth-top ceramic-glass surface. There's some

debate about how easy to clean these surfaces are, and they increase energy use. For safety, an electric cooktop should have controls that indicate which burners are on or still hot.

Halogen and magnetic induction cooktops are still being road tested for the residential market. Both have smooth ceramic-glass tops, use electricity to power up the heat source, and are expensive. A magnetic-induction cooktop, said to be more energy-efficient than a standard electric cooktop, requires flat-bottomed ferrous cookware for the best results; some chefs claim that it rivals gas for instantly controllable and super-high heat. All praise its ability to maintain a low simmer. Halogen cooktops require dark-colored pans for efficient cooking and cook like standard electric cooktops but cost much more.

5 This kitchen fan dates from 1912 and is original to the kitchen. During the remodel it was restored, reglazed, and given chrome plating.

1 Cooktops should be ventilated by a hood or a downdraft vent. Because heat rises, ventilating hoods are more effective and efficient than downdraft systems, which can't always capture steam from tall pots. All ventilation systems require adequately sized fans and large-enough ducts with as straight and short a run to the outside as possible.

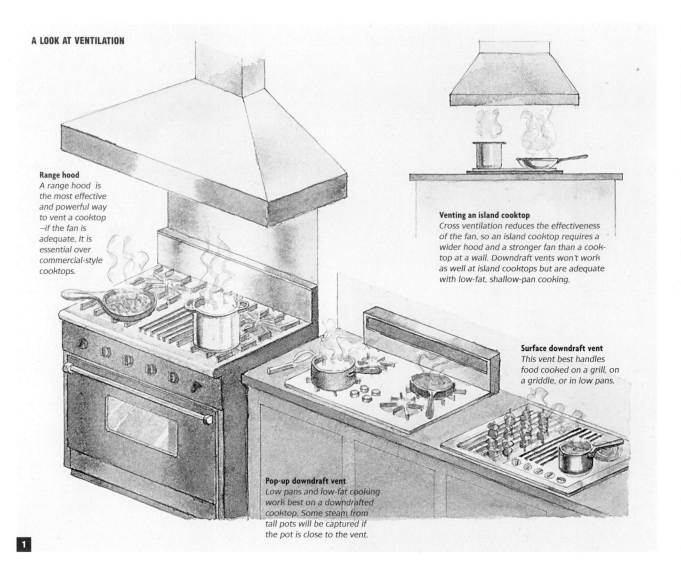

Range hood
A range hood is the most effective and powerful way to vent a cooktop —if the fan is adequate. It is essential over commercial-style cooktops.

Venting an island cooktop
Cross ventilation reduces the effectiveness of the fan, so an island cooktop requires a wider hood and a stronger fan than a cooktop at a wall. Downdraft vents won't work as well at island cooktops but are adequate with low-fat, shallow-pan cooking.

Surface downdraft vent
This vent best handles food cooked on a grill, on a griddle, or in low pans.

Pop-up downdraft vent
Low pans and low-fat cooking work best on a downdrafted cooktop. Some steam from tall pots will be captured if the pot is close to the vent.

1

2 A big, commercial-style range with side-by-side ovens is the focal point of an eat-in kitchen. The microwave also has a place of its own built into the cabinetry.

2

3 Two wide wall ovens provide ample baking space in this family-sized kitchen, and a television takes the top spot. Baking sheets fit in the drawer under the ovens.

4 This professional-style cooktop is as wide as they come. It boasts six burners and a grill. The quilted stainless-steel backsplash and big curved range hood provide necessary restaurant-grade heat resistance and ventilation.

OVEN OPTIONS

Conventional

Most ovens are conventional ovens, also called thermal or radiant ovens, which cook by a combination of radiant energy from a heat source and natural convection from the heated air inside the oven. New cooking methods appear each decade, but conventional ovens work best for everyday cooking. They may be fired by gas or electricity. Gas bakes moister than electric, but many cooks prefer electric for baking because it heats more evenly.

Convection

Convection ovens are a mixed blessing. They cook faster (and so are more energy efficient) but require acclimation—by the cook. Favorite recipes must be modified to have shorter cooking times and lower oven settings. Convection heat may also dry out foods such as cakes and chewy cookies. Its extraordinarily even heat means that chefs can cook a lot of food at once without having to shift pans around to avoid burning. In true convection ovens, the electric heating element is behind the oven cavity and a fan circulates the hot air within the oven, so the food is cooked only by convection, not by the radiant energy from the heating element. The exterior fan shortens the oven's depth, but some convection ovens boast of super-thin space-age insulation that makes the oven wall thinner and the capacity greater.

Combination

A combination conventional/convection oven has the heating element inside the oven and a fan circulates the air. This type doesn't heat as evenly as a true convection oven so it may require food to be adjusted to avoid burning. Convection/microwave ovens alternate the browning capability of the convection oven with the quick internal heating of the microwave, or they can be set to perform one function alone. Such ovens are expensive, and the microwave performance is slower than that of a conventional microwave because the oven space is bigger.

Microwave

The microwave oven is not the kitchen centerpiece it was once forecast to be, but it is still a handy way to defrost, reheat, melt, and pop. How the microwave fits in the kitchen can be tricky. Over the range isn't ideal. It's too hot, the microwave is too high for safe retrieval of hot dishes, and microwave users will collide with cooktop users. Built-in microwave ovens are least obtrusive, but most models are deeper than 15-in. wall cabinets. One possibility is to recess the microwave into a framed box in the stud space so that the face is flush with wall cabinets. Below-countertop and countertop microwave ovens are easier to use by those in wheelchairs. It is not necessarily a bonus to place a microwave low enough for small children to use. If children are capable of using it safely, they will generally be tall enough to comfortably reach a model that's set back on the counter.

Specialty

Specialty ovens include pizza ovens, infrared/halogen ovens, steam ovens, rotisseries, and salamanders. Each of these ovens is costly but serves a specific purpose. One less-expensive specialty model, the warming oven or warming drawer, will appeal to families and frequent entertainers alike.

1 A perfect addition to a Big Sur weekend house, these barbecue and wood-fired pizza ovens are framed with hand-carved limestone.

2 A separate cooktop can work in an island setting, especially if the countertop surrounding it is lowered to make a distinction between the cook's zone and the diners.

There is a difference between true restaurant equipment and restaurant-style, also called professional-style, gear. True restaurant ranges are real scorchers and must stand 3 in. to 4 in. from combustible walls or cabinets. Because it lacks insulation, self-cleaning capability, and a broiler, a restaurant range will often cost less than a restaurant-style residential range, despite its offering of Btus worthy of Hades. Some jurisdictions won't allow their use in homes. Professional-style cooktops and ranges, which are designed specifically for residential use, are insulated to allow them to butt against cabinetry and walls (heat-resistant backsplashes are still a must). Pro-style cooktops also have electronic ignitions, while a true professional cooktop will either have a continuously lit pilot light or its burners must be fired up by a clicker. Above all, whether cooking gear is professional, professional-style, or basic, proper ventilation is vital for a safer, cleaner kitchen.

3 A big family makes use of this double-sized professional-style range with two ovens and eight burners. A continuous grid on the cooktop makes it easier to slide pots from front to back. The tile backsplash is a help for cleanup.

WALL OVENS

Some homeowners prefer the oven to be on a wall so that is easier to access. Wall ovens can be singletons or combined any number of ways. They are available 24 in., 27 in., or 30 in. wide (outside widths, not inside dimensions). Ovens may have different interior dimensions even if outside dimensions are identical. Before buying a narrower wall oven, compare its interior space—its capacity—with your cookware. A 24-in.-wide oven may be able to handle an insulated cookie sheet but not the four-sided baking sheet you use for roasting vegetables. A 27-in.-wide oven can handle just about anything, and a 30-in. oven can take two baking sheets side by side.

COOKING IN AN ALCOVE

4 Tucking a cooktop or range into an alcove can be a smart design move. The walls aid with ventilation and make the hood fan more efficient, and it's easier to shield children and adults from heat, spatters, and hot pots.

5 A gray-green cabinet swells at the base to accommodate a second, wider wall oven.

1 This professional-style range reigns in its own alcove, where it is surrounded by shelves for spices and oils. Ventilation and lighting are easily tucked into the soffit.

Despite the recent boom in the purchase of separate cooktop and oven units, the range, which combines both, remains the most popular cooking appliance. A basic range is less expensive than separate units, although high-end professional-style range prices can leave standard cooktops and wall ovens in the dust. A range offers the benefit of keeping the heat in one part of the kitchen, which can be welcome in a small, one-cook kitchen. Dual-fuel ranges are available with the cook's ideal gas cooktop and the baker's dream, an electric oven. Lovers of vintage kitchens who are not enamored of modern conveniences such as electronic controls and self-cleaning ovens can buy restored or reproduction ranges from pre-1940s that are well built and work beautifully.

Ranges are most often free-standing. They are finished on the sides and can stand alone, at the end of a cabinet run, or even between cabinets (true restaurant ranges have to steer clear of cabinetry). Slide-in and drop-in ranges cost less and don't have finished sides. The basic range is 30 in. wide, but today you can find ranges that stretch up to 5 ft. The width of a range relates to the number of burners and ovens it includes. Be sure that the ovens in a two-oven range are wide enough to handle cookie sheets or a Thanksgiving turkey. For cooktop options, see p. 157. For oven types, see p. 159.

2 A massive professional-style range looks at home in a richly detailed Edwardian-style kitchen.

3 A smaller professional-style range shares one of its countertops with the microwave, which is positioned at a comfortable counter-top height but slides into a cabinet for a built-in look. All microwaves require more depth than is available in the standard 15-in.-deep wall cabinet.

5 Found in this Arts and Crafts–era house, this Magic Chef range was covered with a thick layer of grease and dust. After a thorough cleaning it performs like a new stove.

4 This kitchen in a thoroughly remodeled timber-frame house has two sources of heat: a mighty double-oven professional range and a granite-faced fireplace that's occasionally used for cooking.

6 Why not give the cook a view? The two small windows here provide a relief for the eyes and a respite from cabinetry and appliances. A granite countertop makes a surface that can stand up to hot pots.

STORING POTS & PANS

1 This big range hood can store pot lids along with pots. More pots and pans are stored in an island with open shelves that's just across the aisle from the range.

2 A range-width bar makes a serviceable pot rack for a matching set of pans.

3 A post behind the range is ideal for hanging a set of frequently used Griswold cast-iron skillets.

5 Big, open-front pull-out shelves make great drawers for plates, pots, and pans. It's easier to lift pans from drawers than from inside a cupboard, and the contents of a drawer are much easier to see.

4 Pots hang from ¹/₄-in. stainless-steel rods affixed to a steel framework that also serves to hold lights and enclose a range hood with a copper liner.

6 Cutting boards, pots and pans, and utensils hang from the walls and bright green ceiling joists in the kitchen of sculptor and woodworker Wharton Esherick. The stucco fireplace is for charcoal grilling, while the little gas range handles conventional cooking tasks. A copper sink is set in a cherry countertop finished with clear epoxy.

FLOORS, WALLS, AND CEILINGS

Surrounding all the handsome cabinetry, gleaming appliances, and expanses of countertop are the surfaces that give a kitchen its shape, pin down its style, and set the stage for a livable kitchen.

The time to choose floor, wall, and ceiling finishes is before the cabinets are specified, before plumbing is roughed in, and before electrical boxes are put in place. Your contractor must know how thick the wall will be and if any special surfaces, such as veneer plaster or paneling, will be applied. Flooring materials, especially, must be chosen early in the game because different types of flooring may require different subfloors and have variable thicknesses and edge details. If you can narrow down the category to, say, wood strip flooring, you can take more time to determine the species and pattern you want.

Final finishes—paint, stain, sealants, wallpaper, trim—go on near the end of the building process. A kitchen that's taking shape in three dimensions can't help but look different from the kitchen on paper or even the kitchen in a 3-D computer drawing. Also, the light and quality of space might suggest a different paint than originally specified. All that makes it a good idea to take the advice of a seasoned designer, who has seen how certain colors look together and how space and light interact with specific materials.

CEILINGS are easy to ignore but make a big visual impact on a kitchen when they're given the attention they deserve. The coffered ceiling in this renovated 1885 kitchen looks structural but isn't. Spaces between false beams are painted and glazed with several coats and colors to give the ceiling a rich patina.

FLOORS are a critical element in how a kitchen works and how it wears. Wood, once the floor finish of choice in North America, is seeing a renaissance, thanks to durable polyurethane coatings. This hardwood strip floor is oak, the most popular species for wood flooring.

WALLS in kitchens most often take a back seat to cabinetry and appliances. If a wall is exposed, consider painting it a color other than white. These walls were given what the designer describes as a "rusty-old, Tuscan terra-cotta" color.

FROM THE GROUND UP

1 The floor, walls, and ceiling in this Tucson kitchen suit the Southwest's hot, dry climate. The black-tinted concrete floor is cool in summer and contains radiant heating for winter, and the high, exposed-joist ceiling allows heat to rise. Walls are clear-finished rammed earth, which moderates the summer heat and calls to mind adobe, one of the earliest building materials.

2

2 The wide-board pine floor is original to the kitchen and was gently refinished to retain its richness of character. Throughout the kitchen, walls are painted rich shades of blue, green, and purple as a background for bleached maple cabinets and stainless-steel appliances.

3 A cheerful, fanciful kitchen inspired by Turkish bazaars is finished top to toe with bright, colorful designs. The floor is an inexpensive painted seagrass mat that can easily be pulled up and replaced.

3

4 An existing fir floor takes on a new life with a layer of whitewash, a second layer of stenciled light-green glaze to simulate tiles, and four coats of polyurethane. Wainscoting of painted 3½-in. beadboard gives the new kitchen a durable and handsome wall finish. A tall baseboard balances the chest-high wainscoting.

4

RADIANT HEAT

A kitchen floor is a perfect place for radiant heat. Radiant heat is usually hydronic, meaning that the heat is carried by tubes of water under the floor (electric-cable radiant-heat systems are less efficient and more expensive). The tubes can be run under the subfloor in a kitchen with a wood floor (even an existing wood floor if the subfloor is accessible between joists), or they can be laid on the subfloor and encased in concrete. The concrete can be the finish floor, or it can be a base for tile, stone, or a floating wood floor, which isn't attached to the subfloor. With either method, insulation should be provided below the tubing layer. The concrete-encased method will be more efficient because heat is transferred better through denser materials.

Radiant heat is expensive to install but less expensive to run than most heating systems, and it is supremely comfortable. It is efficient, heats evenly, feels great to cold toes, and does away with the need to blow air—and potential allergens—into the room.

The kitchen floor rarely gets short shrift in the design process because it's obvious that the floor will lay the groundwork for how the kitchen looks and works. A floor is similar to a countertop in its visibility and in its role as stage for making dinner. Instead of supporting the many tasks of chopping vegetables, rolling dough, or serving food, however, a floor supports our bodies, as well as furniture and dropped food and dishes. It must be strong and able to take wear, but it also must be comfortable enough to stand on for long periods. Like a countertop, the floor should be impervious to the occasional big spill, although it may not always resist standing water.

RESILIENT FLOORING

1 Linoleum has made a comeback on kitchen floors. It's soft, durable, and made of natural materials. This linoleum grapevine is inlaid in a field of cork-colored linoleum.

2 Vinyl tile can make a low-cost but elegant floor, as it does here in big, white tiles that highlight the kitchen aisles. This riverside house looks rather like a steamboat on the exterior, so it is fitting that the ceiling is accented by a beadboard cove lit by industrial fixtures.

RESILIENT FLOORING

Resilient flooring is classified as any flexible, thin material that is glued to the subfloor and includes vinyl tile, sheet vinyl, linoleum, and cork. Laminate flooring is rigid and applied more like a floating wood floor (see the drawing below).

Because they are easy to install, vinyl tile and sheet vinyl are the most common kitchen materials. Sheet vinyl has the advantage of being more water-resistant and easier to clean. Both tile and sheet vinyl are available as cushioned vinyl, which has a thinner color layer, and inlaid vinyl, which has a thicker wear layer, a richer, more matte look, and a higher price tag.

Cork is more expensive than most vinyl but it makes a handsome floor. Today's cork tiles can be impregnated with polyurethane for more durability and moisture resistance than their predecessors. Cork's earthy color and overall pattern complement kitchens with lots of wood without looking like wood, and it is a warm counterpoint to plastic-laminate or metal finishes.

Linoleum, still made from natural materials such as wood pulp, cork, and linseed oil, is quiet, durable, and environmentally friendly, but it is fairly expensive, less resistant to moisture, and has a modest palette of colors and patterns.

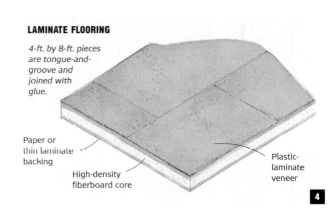

LAMINATE FLOORING

4-ft. by 8-ft. pieces are tongue-and-groove and joined with glue.

Paper or thin laminate backing

High-density fiberboard core

Plastic-laminate veneer

4

3

3 A vinyl-tile floor is easy on the feet and a breeze to maintain and adds character to a kitchen without breaking the bank. The matching checkerboard kitchen table was an auspicious find.

4 Laminate flooring can look like wood or stone, as shown here. It is very durable and resistant to stains and won't gap or buckle. Carefully glued joints are critical to this flooring material's resistance to moisture.

5

5 A sheet-vinyl floor is highly water resistant and comfortable to stand on. This floor is patterned to look like random-width strips of stone.

WOOD FLOORING

1 This eye-catching wood floor was stained with a translucent, red aniline dye to complement the sage-green and lavender-stained wall cabinets. Base cabinets are clear-finished maple.

4 Strips of mahogany flooring record the location of the old walls in a cramped kitchen that was opened up. Diagonal oak strip flooring fills in as a playful indication of where a pantry once was.

2 Hardwood strip flooring makes a warm, comfortable kitchen floor that can also be practical and long-lasting. All it needs is a polyurethane finish, regular vacuuming, and damp (not wet) mopping.

3 Reclaimed, random-width pine boards give an instantly antique appearance to a kitchen in a Shingle-style house on the waterfront.

4

5

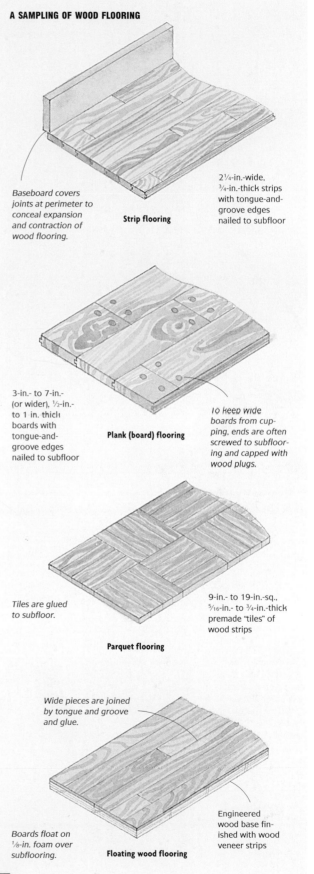

Baseboard covers joints at perimeter to conceal expansion and contraction of wood flooring.

2¼-in.-wide, ¾-in.-thick strips with tongue-and-groove edges nailed to subfloor

Strip flooring

3-in.- to 7-in.- (or wider), ½-in.- to 1 in. thick boards with tongue-and-groove edges nailed to subfloor

To keep wide boards from cupping, ends are often screwed to subflooring and capped with wood plugs.

Plank (board) flooring

Tiles are glued to subfloor.

9-in.- to 19-in.-sq., 5/16-in.- to ¾-in.-thick premade "tiles" of wood strips

Parquet flooring

Wide pieces are joined by tongue and groove and glue.

Boards float on ⅛-in. foam over subflooring.

Engineered wood base finished with wood veneer strips

Floating wood flooring

6

WOOD FLOORING

Wood flooring has covered North American kitchen floors for centuries, while stone and tile are typical in European kitchens. Wood is more abundant on this continent, is durable, beautiful, easy on the feet, and can be finished in a variety of ways. Today's polyurethane coatings can make wood a good choice for kitchens if you vacuum or sweep regularly and wipe up spills quickly. Dogs, kids, and leaky appliances can shorten the life of a floor's finish, and even the wood itself. But another virtue of a wood floor is that it can be refinished over and over.

Most wood floors today are oak, which is strong and has a pronounced grain. Maple and ash are becoming more popular, and exotic woods can be used for accents. Softer woods, such as pine, fir, walnut, and cherry, are too soft to stand up to much wear, although old heartwood pine is denser and is a popular (and expensive) choice for floors in period kitchens.

Nearly all wood flooring comes in 2¼-in., tongue-and-groove strips, but wider and narrower strips are available, as are plank flooring (which is simply 3-in. or wider boards), parquet flooring, and floating wood

flooring, usually made from laminated wood. Strip and plank floors fit together with a tongue-and-groove joint and are then nailed to the subfloor. Traditional parquet flooring was made up of small pieces of solid wood nailed down in geometric patterns, but today's parquet floors are made of preassembled wood tiles that are already glued up in patterns, such as herringbone and basketweave. Parquet tiles are glued down.

Floating wood floors are made of preassembled pieces of laminated wood (also called engineered wood), which is wood veneer laminated to a plywood substrate. Large pieces (6 in. to 8 in. wide and 8 ft. long) are edge-glued together and float on a foam or low-density fiber panel underlayment. A floating wood floor is thin, easy to install, and less affected by humidity than solid wood. Its limitations are a thin wear layer, which can't take more than two or three bouts of refinishing and which shows wear more than solid wood, and its joints, which can be susceptible to water if the edge-gluing is less than perfect.

5 The tile border is an illusion, painted by hand and with stencils on ¼-in. lauan plywood, itself placed on a plywood subfloor. Finished with several coats of polyurethane, it makes a durable, whimsical floor for a kitchen.

6 Strip flooring is the most common type of wood floor. Other options are plank, parquet, and floating wood flooring.

STONE & TILE FLOORING

1 Tile can be cold and hard on the feet, but it can also be warm and inviting, as in this comfortable island kitchen.

2 This limestone-like ceramic tile floor appears to be woven, with spaces between the warp and weft filled with smaller, dark tiles of various shapes and sizes.

3 Unsealed French terra-cotta tiles were heated then coated with boiled linseed oil to seal and darken the tile. This tile has a distinct grain pattern as a result of the way it was worked and extruded in the field. Its smooth surface is finished with an occasional coat of bowling alley wax paste.

TILE AND STONE

Ceramic tile and stone tiles have always made the most durable floors. In the 1600s stone floors were strewn with thick layers of sand, which was replaced often, and rush matting was positioned at main working areas, presumably to cushion the feet and catch spills. Today's stone floors—usually granite, limestone, slate, or marble—are meant to be admired, so they are simply covered with a transparent sealer to prevent staining. Both unglazed tiles and stone require sealing, preferably once before grouting and once after, then periodically. Glazed ceramic tile is completely resistant to staining and needs nothing but regular washing to stay new. If you like the look of stone but not its price tag or its need for a bit more care, consider stone-like ceramic tile, which is made in random sizes and with the color and texture of various types of stone. Choose a non-slip finish for safety.

Tile and stone require strong, stiff floors to carry the weight and to prevent cracking at joints. Tile and stone make fairly thick floors, so it's more difficult to retrofit with tile. The tile or stone itself is $3/8$ in. to $7/8$ in. thick and must be set on concrete, $1/2$-in. backer board, or, rarely, a thick bed of mortar. Setting tile on a $3/4$-in. plywood subfloor is not recommended; add a layer of backer board first.

The downside to such beauty and strength is that a tile floor is hard on feet and brutal to dropped dishes. Nonslip rugs can take the place of the rush mats of the olden days, but rugs aren't as easy to maintain as the floor, defeating the purpose of tile. It's true that tile floors are cold, but this quality can be put to good use for cooling hot pots and baking sheets of cookies (best when there's just one cook in the kitchen), and cool floors feel great in the summer. In cooler months, tile and stone—and concrete—floors can also absorb radiant heat from sunlight coming in through windows and release it slowly after dark. Finally, these dense, hard floors are ideal for radiant-heat systems (see the sidebar on p. 169).

4 This kitchen floor is a simple and striking composition of nine square tiles set between stained wood strips.

5 For a built-in doormat, small, smooth river rocks are set in mortar at the door. Stone-like tiles take over on the rest of the kitchen floor.

6 Small accent tiles are used at the corners of the larger marble tiles. This pattern is more complicated to lay than a checkerboard and has a subtler rhythm.

A STONE THRESHOLD

Small river rocks

CONCRETE FLOORING

1 The curved copper-strip inlay in this concrete floor serves both as an elegant counterpoint to the angular cabinets and as a control joint, to localize any cracking.

2 Most floors in this Maine house are wood, but the hard-working kitchen called for a radiant-heat concrete floor. The concrete was colored by a green pigment troweled into the mix to give it the look of slate without the cost. After curing, the concrete was cut with 4-ft.-square decorative control joints and sealed three times.

CONCRETE FLOORS

Concrete has seen a surge in its use on countertops and floors for good reason. It's as durable as stone and tile but (usually) less expensive. Like stone and unglazed tile, concrete requires a sealer to prevent staining and to make it easy to clean. Concrete absorbs heat like stone and tile and is the consummate flooring material for radiant heat. To top it off, concrete can take on an amazing number of deep colors and rich finishes. Color can be integral to the concrete mix or added after placing by working in powder or by staining.

Concrete work is sloppy, so it's best done in new construction or with plenty of protection in an existing house. Like tile, concrete is heavy, so plan the floor structure accordingly. Another consideration is where to place the joints. Concrete will crack, so cast or cut control joints into the surface where recommended, depending on factors such as the type of concrete and the type of structure supporting it. Make the joints part of the design of the floor, whether by scoring the concrete in even segments or by casting in metal or wood strips in a decorative pattern.

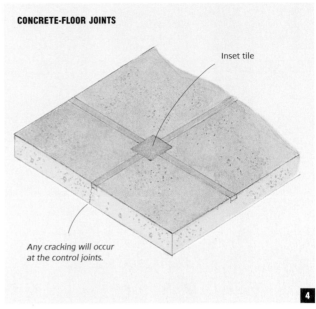

CONCRETE-FLOOR JOINTS

Inset tile

Any cracking will occur at the control joints.

4

3 Initially, the owners of this farmhouse wanted tile floors throughout, but concrete got the nod for its lower cost, ability to incorporate radiant heat, and beauty. The concrete floor received a tint, a sealant, and a waxing. It is scored into rectangular blocks.

5

4 Concrete requires a control joint every 100 sq. ft. or less, depending on thickness and configuration. Joints can be scored directly in the concrete before it cures, or wood or metal strips or inset tiles can be positioned before the concrete is placed.

5 The concrete floor on the top level of this tall but small (884-sq.-ft.) house is finished with a superstrong blue epoxy paint.

WALLS & CEILINGS

1 Interior walls and the soffit are covered with pine sheathing, traditional for un-winterized oceanside cottages but now pricier than drywall. Sheathing is white-washed in flat white paint thinned 50% with water, while the trim received a less diluted white semi-gloss. The soffit delineates the edge of the kitchen and accommodates plumbing lines in this timber-frame house.

2 Formerly a dark room trapped under a solid shed roof, this kitchen is now a bright, family-friendly space thanks to a series of dormers with high windows. The owners spent weeks with paper and crayons testing out colors until they hit on shades of yellow, turquoise, and blue, which cover cabinets, trim, and walls. The curved, arched wall is finished with bead-board, also painted.

3 A mix of slick and rough textures is at home in a new kitchen addition. The floor is vinyl tile, and the stove alcove is finished with brick facing and white subway tile and framed with a hefty wood lintel.

Making a change to the walls and ceilings of an existing kitchen can give it an entirely new lease on life. New paint or wallpaper can be an inexpensive way to make a kitchen brighter or more in keeping with the latest in fashion. Either surface can be the canvas for faux painting or stenciling, and it doesn't necessarily take a professional to do it well.

Consider how colors work in the kitchen. Arts and Crafts master Gustav Stickley thought that kitchens should be cool to balance the heat that's generated. A kitchen that faces north may, on the other hand, benefit from warm colors on the wall. Pale blue is the traditional color of porch and kitchen ceilings in the South because it is said to repel flies. Flies or not, pale blue simply looks fresh and cool in a hot room. Select satin paint, or glossier, and smooth wallpaper textures that are easy to wash and that don't attract grease and fingerprints.

Wall and ceiling finishes can easily be integrated into construction. Painted or stained wood paneling can add warmth and traditional style to a kitchen, and it makes a durable wall finish in a room that generates plenty of grime. Paneling should be designed before trim and cabinets are ordered. Frame-and-panel wainscoting on walls has an elegant, traditional look, while beadboard paneling can provide the look of a farmhouse or coastal cottage. Veneer plaster on blue board is another alternative to drywall. It's generally a more expensive finish than drywall, but it can skim over imperfections in an old house and give walls a more traditional look.

1 The soft yellow color of these walls comes from a pigmented plaster skim coat. The tinted concrete half-wall achieved its silky texture not from finishing but from super-slick formwork.

2 A thick wall of cabinets separates the kitchen from a cathedral-ceilinged living room. The flat kitchen ceiling is accented by rough-hewn ornamental beams.

3 The kitchen in a 1,000-sq.-ft. bungalow needed visual relief, so the owner/designers knocked out the ceiling, installed skylights, finished the underside of the roof structure, and wrapped the now-exposed beams in copper.

4 A wood-paneled ceiling brings warmth and character to a kitchen. It's a more expensive finish than drywall, but it won't crack and doesn't require periodic coats of paint to look its best.

5 In an Adirondack-style house on the West Coast, the kitchen is topped off with rough-hewn white-pine rafters and beams and ponderosa pine ceiling boards.

LIGHT IN
THE KITCHEN

A light, bright kitchen is a delight to be in day or night. How a kitchen is lit makes a tremendous difference in how easy it is to cook, serve, eat, clean up, or just hang out. During the day, sunlight or diffuse daylight adds not only warmth but also atmosphere. Good light is essential in the morning and a boon throughout the rest of the day. When warmth isn't desired but light is, consider seasonal shading by way of overhangs, trees, interior shades or curtains, or all of the above. A window on an east wall will bring in a different quality of light than a window facing north. Make the best of it by window size, configuration, and shading.

As for the kitchen at night, think how stage lighting changes the atmosphere of a set and the countenance of an actor. A variety of light sources and controls will allow for a variety of uses, whether it's time for the whole gang to start chopping vegetables or for mom and dad to sit down at the counter for a quiet meal after the kids are asleep. Focus the most light on where the work is but provide light to brighten the whole kitchen; add accents for special cabinetry or other kitchen elements, or to intensify the space of the kitchen. Kitchens that are open to dining rooms and family rooms benefit from dimmable accent lighting and ambient lighting so that the entire kitchen isn't a black hole but the stacks of dirty pots and pans stay in shadow.

ACCENT LIGHTING adds a spark to a kitchen by lighting objects or walls. Here, a copper sconce highlights the texture of plaster veneer walls.

AMBIENT AND TASK LIGHTING is handled by two copper-shaded, Craftsman-style pendant lights over the kitchen dining table, which sees double duty for food preparation and dining.

TASK LIGHTING for countertops is provided by slim under-cabinet fluorescent lights. Each light is shielded from view by an apron attached to the shelf edge.

RECESSED-CAN fixtures in the soffit over the sink offer task lighting for cleanup and meal preparation and also act as accent lights for glasses and dishware on recessed shelves.

WINDOWS bring daylight to kitchen tasks and provide a connection to the outdoors. This one is set in a thick wall, making room for a window garden.

KITCHEN WINDOWS

1 The fixed transom windows were custom-built to match the manufactured casement windows below. A broad overhang keeps direct sun out but lets plenty of light in. To supplement light from the windows, lights are fitted into the beam, which is actually a pair of 2x10s with a plenum between that accommodates electrical conduit, a waste line from upstairs, and a heating duct.

2 A salvaged window enjoys a second life in a bay added behind a stainless-steel kitchen sink set in a slate countertop (right). By way of an adjustable counterweight—a procedure borrowed from movie sets—the window opens fully to make the kitchen counter an inside/outside space (below). At the outer corners of the new bay are two stacks of glass shelves that hold potted plants (left).

Windows both extend the space of a kitchen and clarify the objects and space within it. They can also allow for desirable heat gain and provide ventilation. A rule of thumb is that the area of a kitchen's windows should be at least 10% of the floor area. That means a 15-ft.-square kitchen should have at least two 3-ft. by 4-ft. windows. For maximum energy efficiency, use wood, aluminum-clad wood, vinyl-clad wood, or vinyl windows. Insulating glass, preferably with low-E coating, will easily pay for itself in most climates by keeping cold or heat out longer than single-layer glazing.

1 This big, 40-light arched window frames a breathtaking view and brings abundant light into the kitchen in a Shingle-style oceanside house. Three rectangular tilt-turn sash can let in ocean breeze. The pendant fixture over the sink has a halophane-glass shade, which magnifies and disperses light beautifully and efficiently.

3 This easy-to-open, center-pivot window set in a large bay would be ideal behind a sink, where the deep tile sill can house a potted kitchen garden. Windows are Port Orford cedar, which is decay-resistant.

2 Daylight comes into this south-facing kitchen in two forms: directly through a center single-light window over the sink and indirectly through translucent fiberglass panels divided like *shoji* screens. The diffuse light brightens the workspace without glare.

4 Beams are exposed beneath a skylight over the sink in a Martha's Vineyard house. Two decorative pendants provide task lighting for washing up. The thick wall around the window opening is beveled to let in more light. The two outer windows are operable.

SKYLIGHTS

A skylight can add wonderful, diffuse light to a kitchen any time of year, but it also has the potential to make it unbearably hot in the summer. A skylight placed at the edge of a room provides more light because the incoming light bounces off the wall. In hot climates, don't situate skylights toward the south or west unless they can be easily shaded during the afternoon. A skylight in the south can actually help cool a kitchen if it is easily opened (and screened), because the hot air will just rise up through the skylight like a chimney. In cold months, sunlight from a skylight (or tall windows) falling on a stone, tile, or concrete floor warms the floor, which then radiates the heat during the cooler night.

5 Adding a shed-roofed chunk to a San Francisco Bay area house brings light and color to a formerly dark, cramped kitchen. Skylights reach across the kitchen to illuminate the open shelves.

EAST, WEST, WHICH IS BEST (FOR A WINDOW)?

In colder climates, limit windows on the north side to avoid heat loss. But north light is always diffuse and is good for working at a desk or counter without glare.

NORTH

The afternoon sun can be harsh and hot, so shading by way of deciduous trees and window shades is critical on a west wall.

East windows are a boon for morning kitchen use. Provide window shading (shades, curtains, interior shutters) in warmer climates if desired.

WEST

EAST

In climates with more cloudy than sunny days, windows can be bigger.

Provide window shading, roof overhangs, or deciduous-tree shade at the south windows, whether windows are in wall plans or in bays.

South-facing windows are ideal for window gardens. Provide shade in summer months by way of blinds or roof overhangs.

South-facing windows are best for solar heating during cold months.

SOUTH

6 If possible, situate your kitchen to take advantage of light and breezes. In an existing kitchen, windows can be moved, reconfigured, or shaded to suit your kitchen workings.

1 This kitchen shares light and space with the living room and a four-level stairway. Although the kitchen itself has no windows, east light from a window wall opposite the kitchen floods the space with morning light. Small and large pendant lights, under-cabinet fixtures, and recessed cans brighten the kitchen at night.

2 Fiberglass skylights are twice as insulating as standard double glazing and provide diffuse, not glaring, light. A clear, greenhouse-type skylight over the counter faces north; again, no glare. The glass-to-glass corner visually takes the kitchen out to the trees.

Windows on two walls seem to make light that's brighter and more diffuse than the light that comes from windows facing one direction. But even a single window can make a kitchen seem larger. High windows and corner windows can bring more light into the kitchen, too, because light bounces off the adjacent wall or the ceiling. Windows with sills that are close to the countertop add light to the workspace, and windows can even be placed in the backsplash space, between wall and base cabinets. Unless the window trim and sash are waterproof, it's best not to bring a window down low over the sink. If light is needed but the view is bad, use glass block, frosted glass, or heavy-duty plastic to let in light but maintain privacy.

WINDOW PLACEMENT

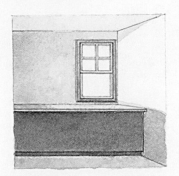

A window placed close to a light-colored wall (above), ceiling (below), or countertop will increase the amount of light in the room because the light bounces off the adjacent surface.

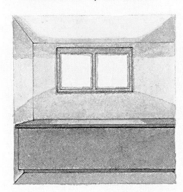

A room with windows on at least two walls will have more even daylighting.

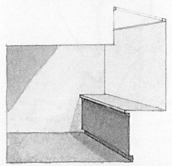

A skylight at the edge of a room can be placed to bounce light off one wall.

3 Thick walls in a carriage house-turned-residence call for a traditional in-swinging window. The bleached-maple wall cabinets, which align with this window and a flanking twin, are positive counterpoints to the deep window.

3

5

4 Window placement greatly affects the quality of light coming into a kitchen.

5 Two types of window have two different uses. The large, arched window faces a water garden and path to the front door, and a stained-glass window behind the range adds both light and beauty to the kitchen. This window faces a small court just outside the front door.

6 Two stacked, multi-light garage doors were less expensive than manufactured windows and provide an 800-sq.-ft. one-room house with a soaring view of the woods. The upper door is fixed, but the lower door raises up for access and breezes.

4

6

LIGHTING

1 A shop-built sconce with translucent panels is a simple, handsome way to provide accent and ambient lighting in the kitchen.

2 This copper wall sconce is one of two in a kitchen influenced by the Craftsman style. Its function is to provide ambient light and to accent the soft texture of the plaster-veneered wall.

Many older kitchens aren't bright enough after the sun goes down. The most pleasant kitchen lighting comes from several sources. Lighting designers classify kitchen lighting as either task lighting, general—or ambient—lighting, or accent lighting. That doesn't mean you need three different types of fixtures; many light fixtures can handle more than one lighting job at a time.

3 Count the types of lighting in this kitchen in a new bungalow-style house. First, there's natural light, which comes from clerestory windows, which bring in diffuse light, and from the window behind the kitchen sink. Then there's the lighting fixtures, which include slim under-cabinet fluorescents, handsome surface-mounted incandescent fixtures under the soffit, and two ambient and two bright Arts and Crafts–style pendants to provide ambient and task lighting.

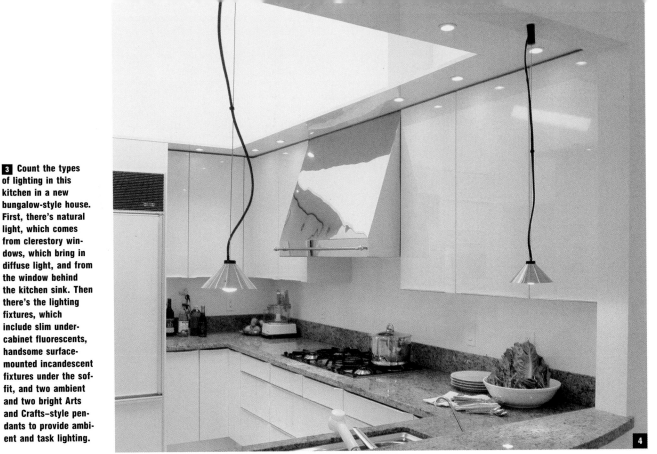

4

4 An almost room-sized skylight pumps plenty of light into this kitchen, while tiny halogen puck lights sparkle from an encircling soffit. Delicate curved pendant fixtures provide task and ambient lighting to the bar counter.

5 Lighting fixtures are available for almost every surface and every conceivable task in a kitchen. When choosing a fixture, keep in mind how it will look during the day.

GUIDELINES FOR LIGHTING THE KITCHEN

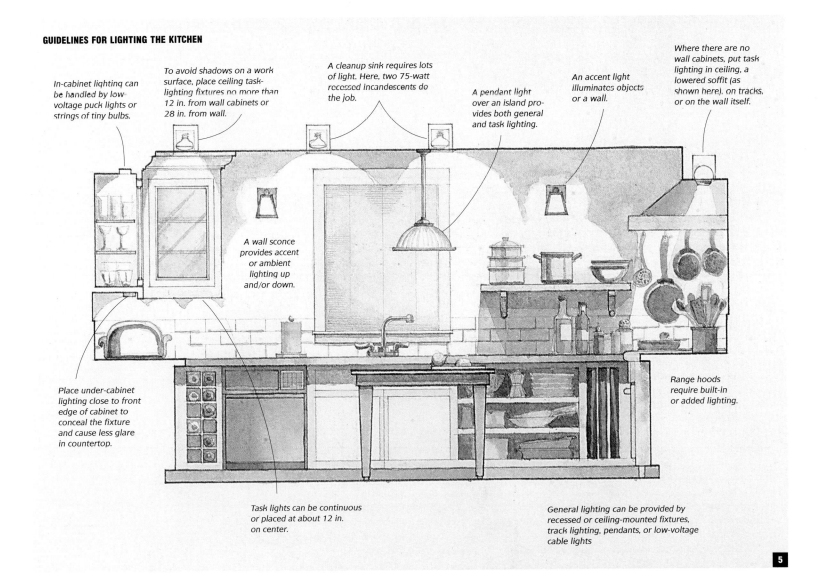

In-cabinet lighting can be handled by low-voltage puck lights or strings of tiny bulbs.

To avoid shadows on a work surface, place ceiling task-lighting fixtures no more than 12 in. from wall cabinets or 28 in. from wall.

A cleanup sink requires lots of light. Here, two 75-watt recessed incandescents do the job.

A pendant light over an island provides both general and task lighting.

An accent light illuminates objects or a wall.

Where there are no wall cabinets, put task lighting in ceiling, a lowered soffit (as shown here), on tracks, or on the wall itself.

A wall sconce provides accent or ambient lighting up and/or down.

Place under-cabinet lighting close to front edge of cabinet to conceal the fixture and cause less glare in countertop.

Range hoods require built-in or added lighting.

Task lights can be continuous or placed at about 12 in. on center.

General lighting can be provided by recessed or ceiling-mounted fixtures, track lighting, pendants, or low-voltage cable lights

1 These whimsical pendant lights were crafted from aluminum tubing by a local artist. Each takes a 60-watt candelabra bulb.

2 Martha's Vineyard seems the appropriate site for a kitchen with a pierced-copper fish chandelier.

3 A swooping stained-glass pendant light adds a touch of light to the workspace and a lot of ambience to the kitchen.

4 Low-voltage halogen lights strung across the kitchen provide dramatic lighting. Two pendants handle work at the sink island. The range hood has built-in halogen lights over the cooktop. Because the kitchen faces abundant windows in the living room, only clerestory windows are added to the kitchen to allow light to glance along the ceiling and allow views of treetops.

LIGHTING OPTIONS

Task lighting should provide about three-quarters of the light in your kitchen. Task lighting works best if it's positioned in front of you so that your body doesn't make a shadow over the workspace. This is accomplished best by under-cabinet lighting, perhaps supplemented by recessed-can ceiling fixtures 10 in. to 12 in. from the wall cabinet. Under-cabinet lights can be low-voltage halogen "puck" lights or track lights; a less expensive and cooler way to light the countertop is with slimline fluorescent fixtures (go for warm-white bulbs). While puck lights can be centered under a wall cabinet, it's best to put incandescent lighting behind a lip at the outer edge of the cabinet to minimize glare and better hide the fixture. In kitchens without wall cabinets, task lighting can be supplied by recessed or ceiling-mounted fix-tures, placed 12 in. to 28 in. from the wall. A well-lit sink will have a 40-watt fluorescent or two 75-watt incandescent fixtures. Cook-tops require similar treatment.

General lighting lights the space, either from ceiling-mounted fixtures, recessed-can fixtures, pendant lighting, or track lighting, a handy method of providing task, general, or accent lighting that is coming back into fashion with a variety of good-looking fixtures. Good task lighting may provide enough general lighting by itself, but it's a plus to have more than one type of fixture. Low-voltage halogen lights on cables add sparkle and ambience, but they won't light up a cutting board sufficiently. Recessed cans are commonly used for general lighting, but don't count on them for all your lighting needs. An abundance of recessed cans will pock the ceiling during the day and leave the ceiling plane dark at night. Recessed cans with white or mirrored interiors will reflect more light and won't look so dark in daylight. Consider eyeball trims that can direct the light or sur-face-mounted frosted lenses, which add a bit of light to the ceiling. Make sure that cans are venti-lated; insulated ceilings require fixtures that are rated for that situation.

Accent lighting is optional, but it can add drama to a kitchen and even serve alone when task and general lights have been switched off. Glass-door cabinets are perfect for low-voltage accent lights. Indirect lighting above wall cabinets can wash the wall and ceiling and be strong enough to provide general lighting.

Lighting an island or table can be done with general or task light-ing and is handled by recessed or surface-mounted ceiling fixtures or by pendant lights. If the pen-dant light has a translucent shade or is open at the top, it will add light to the ceiling. An opaque shade will direct light only on the island or table. Keep the bottom of the pendant at about 36 in. above an island and 30 in. above a dining table—higher if the ceiling is higher—and make sure that it is well within the boundaries of the table or island so no one can bump it. If the table or island is a workspace, make the light brighter. A 120-watt incandescent fixture or a 40-watt fluorescent fixture should suffice.

1 Pendant lights in the kitchen have halogen lamps that are magnified by thin, heat-resistant, translucent plastic disks; glassware in the open cabinets reflects the halogen's sparkle. The lights over the tile wall just outside the kitchen are inexpensive incandescent garden fixtures turned horizontal.

2 Under-cabinet lights can be slimline fluorescent fixtures or low-voltage halogen "puck" lights.

3 The existing windows in this kitchen were too low for base cabinets, so a tiled niche was added to provide visual delight behind the wash-up sink. Lights behind the arch illuminate the mosaic and the sink.

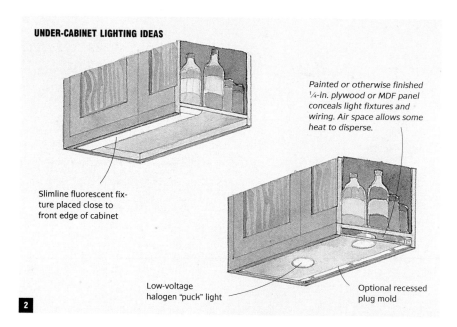

UNDER-CABINET LIGHTING IDEAS

Slimline fluorescent fixture placed close to front edge of cabinet

Painted or otherwise finished ¼-in. plywood or MDF panel conceals light fixtures and wiring. Air space allows some heat to disperse.

Low-voltage halogen "puck" light

Optional recessed plug mold

Your lighting requirements will depend on the color and surface texture of the finishes in your kitchen. Kitchens with dark or matte surfaces will demand more light than those with light or shiny surfaces. Shiny countertops will benefit from frosted fixtures or bulbs, which won't produce as much glare as clear bulbs. Put incandescent or halogen lights on dimmers, if possible. Dimmers create a flexible lighting plan and extend the life of the bulb.

4 An antique painted-plaster light fixture casts a bright light with no glare over a kitchen island.

5 Pendant lights are ideal for lighting a kitchen island, as in this Adirondack-style house. These pendants are small enough to keep from getting in the way of views and heads, yet their white-glass shades punch up the light for food-prep tasks.

6 This handsome stained-maple structure is one part sculpture, one part respository for shelves (spice shelves fit into the other side), and one part light fixture, including fluorescent strips for task lighting and tiny twinkle lights around the perimeter for ambience. Slanted sides were inspired by the owners' collection of Mayan art.

BULB BASICS

The lighting industry calls bulbs *lamps*, but bulbs will do here. Although the broad category of **incandescent** bulbs includes any bulb with a filament, including tungsten and halogen bulbs, we think of incandescent light as being the standard light bulb; it's called an A-type bulb. Other incandescent bulbs found in houses are the R and the PAR, which are wider and brighter (you'll find them in recessed-can light fixtures). An incandes-cent bulb doesn't cost much, but it is much more expensive to run than a fluorescent bulb because the bulb life is so short and its light output per watt is less. Still, people like incandescent lighting because its warm color is flattering to people and food. Incandescent lights are also easy to dim. Frosted bulbs make light diffuse, good in a kitchen with shiny surfaces such as granite and stainless steel. Clear bulbs can be focused.

A **fluorescent** bulb is four times as efficient as an incandescent and lasts at least ten times longer. It makes an even, cooler light that doesn't diminish with age as much as an incandescent. It needs a ballast, which can be remote to eliminate the buzz, and it is difficult to dim. Look for warm-white bulbs, which are closer to incandescent white than the cool blue-green commonly associated with commercial fluorescent lighting.

Halogen fixtures make a bright, white light and while the bulbs last seven times as long as a standard incandescent and use less energy, they are much more expensive initially than incandescent. Halogen fixtures require a transformer. A prime drawback to halogen is that it can get very hot. Low-voltage halogen fixtures, such as under-cabinet puck lights, don't generate quite as much heat, but they still warm up the bottom of a wall cabinet.

There's no end to information about kitchens, from design to construction. Here are books, magazines, and associations that you will find especially helpful in your search. You'll find sources for good kitchen design, for designers, for guidelines to historic styles, for product literature, and for how kitchens and components are built. I haven't singled out the semi-annual kitchen magazines on the grocery-store rack; check them for the latest appliances as well as other kitchen products. Finally, there's the Internet, a gold mine of the latest information, if you can find the vein.

Designing a Kitchen

Not all of these books are exclusively about kitchens, but the insight they give into the design of a house can't help but apply to the most important room in the home.

Alexander, Christopher, et al. *A Pattern Language*. New York: Oxford University Press, 1977.
The patterns in this book are for making towns, neighborhoods, houses, and kitchens. Examples of patterns that could pertain to your kitchen are "Farmhouse Kitchen" and "Windows on Two Walls." One intriguing pattern is a continuous shelf 9 in. to 15 in. deep that runs throughout set deep into a thick wall and interrupted periodically by window alcoves and cabinets. This dense book has no index, but it is endlessly fascinating and inspiring in its trust that people can make their lives better by building better places.

Clark, Sam. *The Motion-Minded Kitchen*. Boston: Houghton Mifflin, 1983.
Clark describes his ergonomically focused, pro-open-shelf method of designing a kitchen. Work sequences provide the driving force behind his kitchen layout.

Goldbeck, David. *The Smart Kitchen*. Woodstock, N.Y.: Ceres Press, 1989.
This writer presents his cooking-based point of view of how a kitchen should operate and what materials he suggests avoiding (such as tile flooring); the book contains some unusual details, such as using a skid for traction and to stretch the cook's reach.

Kimball, Herrick. *The Kitchen Consultant: A common-sense guide to kitchen remodeling*. Newtown, Conn.: The Taunton Press, 1998.
A sensible and detailed look at the parts of a kitchen, written by a remodeling contractor with 20-plus years of experience.

Krasner, Deborah. *Kitchens for Cooks*. New York: Viking Penguin, 1994.
Whether or not you make use of the somewhat complex point of view about kitchen design in this book, take a look at the kitchen photographs. All the kitchens are owned by serious cooks.

Moore, Charles, Gerald Allen & Donlyn Lyndon. *The Place of Houses*. New York: Holt, Rinehart and Winston, 1974.
For people who want to get truly involved in the design of their houses or additions, this 1970s book remains a classic. Three renowned architects analyze what makes certain houses agreeable, then discuss ways to consider rooms to live in, machines that serve life, and inhabitants' dreams. The book ranges from the theoretical to the practical, and a detailed questionnaire helps the reader consider the ideal paths of water, air, food, dirt, dishes, cars, and children.

Rand, Ellen and Florence Perchuk. *Complete Book of Kitchen Design*. Yonkers, N.Y.: Consumer Reports Books, 1991.
This book has minimal visuals and doesn't have the very latest in kitchen gear, but its review of appliances is thorough and useful.

Rybczynski, Witold. *Home: A Short History of an Idea*. New York: Viking Penguin, 1986.
This is a highly readable and thoughtful book about the history of the home and comfort over the last thousand years, with note taken both of the design of the house and of particular domestic inventions. Rybczynski observes that "the kitchen does not function like an office; if anything, it is more like a workshop. Tools should be out in the open...near those places where the work is done...."

Thallon, Rob. *Graphic Guide to Interior Details for Builders and Designers*. Newtown, Conn.: The Taunton Press, 1996.
Thallon explains with text and many architectural details all the finishes found inside buildings. Particularly useful for kitchens are the chapters devoted to cabinet and countertop materials, finishes, and installations.

Thomas, Steve and Philip Langdon. *This Old House Kitchens*. Boston: Little, Brown, 1992.
Read this book for useful information about heating alternatives, cabinet construction, and old-house fixes.

Tolpin, Jim. *Building Traditional Kitchen Cabinets*. Newtown, Conn.: The Taunton Press, 1994.
You don't have to own a single tool to find this book handy. It includes informative charts, such as one in the chapter on finishes, which lists cabinet finishes by type, generic name, ease of repair, and resistance to moisture, stains, abrasion, and fading.

Building a Kitchen

These resources are for anyone who wants to have a hand in the nitty-gritty details in a kitchen, whether by sweat equity or as an educated client.

Kimball, Herrick. *Making Plastic Laminate Countertops*. Newtown, Conn.: The Taunton Press, 1996.

Kimball, Herrick. *Refacing Cabinets: Making an Old Kitchen New*. Newtown, Conn.: The Taunton Press, 1997.

The following are articles from *Fine Homebuilding* magazine, published by The Taunton Press, Newtown, Conn. (search their website at www.taunton.com for more articles):

"Installing Kitchen Cabinets" by Tom Law, 85:48-52

"Installing European Cabinets" by Tom Santarsiero, 85:53

"Kitchen Cabinets from Components" by Sven Hanson & Joel Wheeler, 91:74-79

"Hybrid Cabinet Construction" by Jim Tolpin, 74:74-78

"Refacing Kitchen Cabinets" by Rex Alexander, 81:72-76

"Another Option: Pressure-sensitive Veneer" by Herrick Kimball, 81:76-77

"Site-Built Kitchen" by Tony Simmonds, 79: 76-79

"Hide that Ugly Refrigerator" by Rex Alexander, 108:72-73

PERIOD KITCHENS

Calloway, Stephen, and Elizabeth Cromley (Eds.). *The Elements of Style.* **New York: Simon & Schuster, 1996.**
An excellent guide for researching hardware, trim, lighting, flooring, and wallpaper styles for a period kitchen. As the subtitle says, this is a "practical encyclopedia of interior architectural details from 1485 to the present." This big, expensive book (published in England but containing American styles, too) is packed with tiny drawings and photos of parts of houses. Color-coded tabs allow you to select particular elements, from kitchen stoves to doors to ceilings and walls, and to see how those elements were designed in particular periods, such as American Victorian and Arts and Crafts.

Old House Journal
(www.oldhousejournal.com)
If you are interested in period kitchens, this magazine and its website will guide you in the right direction. Back issues include articles about historically accurate cabinet proportions, Arts and Crafts tiles, vintage stoves, and reproduction lighting.

Traditional Building
(www.traditional-building.com)
Subtitled "The Professional's Source for Historical Products," this big magazine is made up of a few articles paired with charts of related products, addresses, and characteristics, plus an abundance of advertisements grouped by division.

ACCESSIBLE KITCHENS

Wylde, Margaret A., Adrian Baron-Robbins and Sam Clark. *Building for a Lifetime: The Design and Construction of Fully Accessible Homes.* **Newtown, Conn.: The Taunton Press, 1994.**

ENVIRONMENTALLY FRIENDLY KITCHEN PRODUCTS

Berthold-Bond, Annie. *The Green Kitchen Handbook.* **New York: HarperCollins, 1997.**
The bulk of this book is about buying and preparing food that contributes to health and a clean environment. There's a long chapter at the end called "The Ecological Kitchen" that describes how to wash foods and equipment without toxic chemicals, how to purchase and use big

and small appliances to save energy, and how to deal with garbage.

Hermannsson, John. *The Green Building Resource Guide.* **Newtown, Conn.: The Taunton Press, 1997.**
A compilation of manufacturers and suppliers of products and services that deal with environmentally friendly materials, such as formaldehyde-free hardboard.

ASSOCIATIONS AND AGENCIES

National Kitchen and Bath Association 687 Willow Grove St., Hackettstown, NJ 07840; (800) 4100-NKBA (www.nkba.org)
NKBA will send you a list of Certified Kitchen Designers (CKD) in your area. The list is published on line, too. Not all designers belong to this organization, just as not all architects belong to the American Institute of Architects.

Architectural Woodwork Institute 13924 Braddock Rd., P.O. Box 1550, Centreville, VA 22020; (703) 222-1100 (www.awinet.org)
Contact this association for information about cabinet-construction standards.

KITCHENS ON THE WEB

I've found that casting about on the Internet for kitchen information will land about as many old boots as it does keepers, but it's fun fishing. Practically every manufacturer of anything that goes in a kitchen has a website, so if you know a manufacturer's name, just type it in as the keyword in your favorite search engine. Here are just a few of the sites to try; there are untold others waiting to be found.

Appliances
Look up "kitchen appliances" on your favorite search engine and you'll find a mishmash of sites. One site I found interesting was **www.kitchensoup.com**, the site of an online kitchenware company that sells among other things Boos maple tables and carts, Imperial ranges, and wire shelving. Some appliance companies will pop up by this method, such as the small company **Sunfrost**, which makes a highly efficient refrigerator with two cooling systems and no fans. Also try **www.companyname.com** for quicker access; it usually works. Finally, check out the next two sites for appliances:

www.appliance.com
This is the website of *Appliance* magazine. Click on the "Consumer Connection" to find both a comprehensive, up-to-date list of appliance manufacturers and a raft of short articles about choosing and operating appliances.

www.homeappliances.com
On this site, search for a type of appliance and you'll see a list of manufacturers (and links to their sites), a list of special promotions, and links to dealers near you.

www.bauerdesign.com
This is just one website offered by a designer, but this one is particularly nicely done. It's whimsical but informative.

www.consumerreports.org
If you want to get into this site, you must subscribe online. In past online issues, *Consumer Reports* has published results of testing basic appliances, cabinets, and countertops.

www.epa.gov/OGWDW/drinklink.html
This is the site of the Safe Drinking Water Hotline of the Environmental Protection Agency (EPA). If you can't get online or prefer the phone, call (800) 426-4791 for information about water purification systems.

www.lighting-inc.com
This site has an ever-increasing list of lighting manufacturers' addresses (it's billed as the World's Greatest).

www.taunton.com
Go to the *Fine Homebuilding* site and read (or join in) the "Breaktime Discussion Pages" for talk about various building dilemmas (press CTRL-F to do a keyword search). Then peruse "Sites to See" for links to external websites compiled and annotated by the *Fine Homebuilding* magazine staff. Also view "Cooks Talk" at *Fine Cooking*'s site for any discussion about appliances and "Sites to See" for links to manufacturers' sites.

www.traditional-building.com
See "Period Kitchens" above for a description of *Traditional Building* magazine. This website is handy because it links directly to many product manufacturers. Select a product category, such as "Plumbing Fixtures and Hardware," to find links to manufacturers and suppliers.

GREAT KITCHEN DESIGNS

pp. 6-7 DESIGN: Joseph Stevens, Carmel, CA; CABINETRY: Ambrose Pollack, Big Sur, CA; PHOTO: © The Taunton Press, Inc.

pp. 8-9 #1 DESIGN: Fu-Tung Cheng and Frank Lee, Cheng Design, Berkeley, CA; PHOTO: © The Taunton Press, Inc.; #2 DESIGN: Robert Orr, Robert Orr and Associates, New Haven, CT; PHOTO: © The Taunton Press, Inc.; #3 DESIGN: John and Nancy Carney, Carney Architects, Jackson, WY; PHOTO: © The Taunton Press, Inc.; #4 DESIGN: Lou Ann Bauer, ASID, Bauer Interior Design, San Francisco, CA; PHOTO: David Duncan Livingston; #5 DESIGN: Rolf Kielman, Truex Cullins & Partners Architects, Burlington, VT; PHOTO: Becky Luigart-Stayner

pp. 10-11 #1 DESIGN: Joseph Stevens, Carmel, CA; PHOTO: © The Taunton Press, Inc.; #2 DESIGN: John Silverio, Lincolnville, ME; PHOTO: © The Taunton Press, Inc.; #3 DESIGN: McKee Patterson, AIA, Austin Patterson Disston Architects, Southport, CT; CABINETRY: Owen Gardella, Manitou Construction, Roxbury, CT; PHOTO: John Kane; #4 DESIGN: Kaehler/Moore Architects, Greenwich, CT; PHOTO: Durston Saylor; #5 DESIGN: Jonathan Livingston, San Francisco, CA; PHOTO: © The Taunton Press, Inc.

pp. 12-13 #1 DESIGN: Ron Berger, Shutesbury, MA; PHOTO: © The Taunton Press, Inc.; #2 DESIGN: Daniel Wing and Dina Dubois, Corinth, VT; PHOTO: Joanne Kellar Bouknight; #3 DESIGN: Victoria Holland, Bellevue, WA; PHOTO: © The Taunton Press, Inc.; #4 DESIGN: Lou Ann Bauer, ASID, Bauer Interior Design, San Francisco, CA; PHOTO: Andrew McKinney; #5 DESIGN: Frederic Schwartz, New York, NY; PHOTO: Regina Schrambling

pp. 14-15 #1 DESIGN: Ken Foster, Austin, TX; PHOTO: © The Taunton Press, Inc.; #2 DESIGN: Bentel & Bentel Architects/Planners, Locust Valley, NY; CABINETRY: DAMCA, College Point, NY; PHOTO: Eduard Hueber; #3 DESIGN: Michael Hauptman, Brawer & Hauptman Architects, Philadelphia, PA; KITCHEN: Peter Cardamone, Bluebell Kitchens, Springhouse, PA; PHOTO: Barry Halkin; #4 DESIGN: William E. Roesner, Newton Centre, MA; PHOTO: © The Taunton Press, Inc.

pp. 16-17 #1 DESIGN: Sloane M. Chambers, Manchester, ME; PHOTO: © The Taunton Press, Inc.; #2 DESIGN: Derek Van Alstine, Santa Cruz, CA; PHOTO: © The Taunton Press, Inc.; #3 DESIGN: Peter Cardamone, Bluebell Kitchens, Springhouse, PA; PHOTO: Baruch Schwartz; #4 DESIGN: Cecilia Campa, Becker/Zeyco Kitchens, San Francisco, CA; PHOTO: David Duncan Livingston

pp. 18-19 #1 DESIGN: Louis Mackall, Breakfast Woodworks, Guilford, CT; PHOTO: © The Taunton Press, Inc.; #2 DESIGN: Richard Lear, Richard Lear Designs, Southampton, NY; CABINETRY: Peter Craz, Craz Woodworking, Holbrook, NY; PHOTO: Roger Tully; #3 DESIGN: Bentel & Bentel Architects/Planners, Locust Valley, NY; PHOTO: Eduard Hueber; #4 DESIGN: William Dutcher, Berkeley, CA; PHOTO: © The Taunton Press, Inc.

pp. 20-21 #1 DESIGN: Martha B. Finney and Garrett Finney; Philadelphia, PA; PHOTO: © The Taunton Press, Inc.; #2 DESIGN: Cecilia Campa, Becker/Zeyco Kitchens, San Francisco, CA; PHOTO: David Duncan Livingston; #3 DESIGN: Philip S. Sollman, Bellefonte, PA; PHOTO: © The Taunton Press, Inc.; #4 DESIGN: Ernie Rose, Bon Air, VA; PHOTO: © The Taunton Press, Inc.

pp. 22-23 #1 DESIGN: Robert H. Hersey; San Francisco, CA; PHOTO: © The Taunton Press, Inc.; #2 DESIGN: David Borenstein, Red Hood, NY; PHOTO: © The Taunton Press, Inc.

pp. 24-25 #1 DESIGN: Brendan R. Coburn; PHOTO: © The Taunton Press, Inc.; #2 PHOTO: courtesy Plain & Fancy Custom Cabinetry; #3 DESIGN: Michael McNamara, Blue Sky Design, Hornby Island, BC, Canada; PHOTO: © The Taunton Press, Inc.

pp. 26-27 #1 DESIGN: Robert Orr, Robert Orr and Associates, New Haven, CT; PHOTO: © The Taunton Press, Inc.; #2 DESIGN: Susan N. Smith and Ernst A. Benzien, Homeworks Associates, Santa Barbara, CA; PHOTO: © The Taunton Press, Inc.; #3 DESIGN: William E. Roesner, Newton Centre, MA; PHOTO: © The Taunton Press, Inc.; #4 DESIGN: Michaela Mahady and Wayne Branum, Mulfinger, Susanka, Mahady & Partners, Stillwater, MN; PHOTO: © The Taunton Press, Inc.; #5 DESIGN: John Douglas, Phoenix, AZ; PHOTO: Mark Boisclair; #6 DESIGN: Ross Chapin, Whidbey Island, WA; PHOTO: © The Taunton Press, Inc.

pp. 28-29 #1 DESIGN: Ernie Rose, Bon Air, VA; PHOTO: © The Taunton Press, Inc.; #2 DESIGN: Lou Ann Bauer, ASID, Bauer Interior Design, San Francisco, CA; PHOTO: Andrew McKinney; #3 DESIGN: Sarah Susanka, Mulfinger, Susanka, Mahady & Partners, Minneapolis, MN; PHOTO: © The Taunton Press, Inc.; #4 DESIGN: Bob and Jane Blosser, Sonoma, CA; PHOTO: Andrew McKinney; #5 DESIGN: Patricia Swalander, Calgary, Alberta, Canada; PHOTO: David Duncan Livingston

pp. 30-31 #1 DESIGN: Jan Regis, Binns Designer Kitchens and Baths, Pickering, ON, Canada; CONSTRUCTION: Colin Bird, Toronto, ON, Canada; PHOTO: David Duncan Livingston; #2 DESIGN: Bill Mastin, Oakland, CA; PHOTO: © The Taunton Press, Inc.; #3 DESIGN: Robert Orr, Robert Orr and Associates, New Haven, CT; PHOTO: © The Taunton Press, Inc.; #4 DESIGN: Kaehler/Moore Architects, Greenwich, CT; CABINETRY: Coastal Millworks, Bridgeport, CT; PHOTO: Durston Saylor; #5 DESIGN: Bentel & Bentel Architects/ Planners, Locust Valley, NY; CABINETRY: Boos Custom Woodworking, Plainview, NY; PHOTO: Eduard Hueber

p. 32-33 #1 DESIGN: Arnelle Kase, Barbara Scavullo Design, San Francisco, CA; PHOTO: David Duncan Livingston; #2 DESIGN: Sharon Tyler Hoover, Fayetteville, AR; PHOTO: © The Taunton Press, Inc.; #3 DESIGN: Walter Koch, Earlysville, VA; PHOTO: © The Taunton Press, Inc.; #4 PHOTO: David Duncan Livingston

pp. 34-35 #1 DESIGN: Brad Sills, Whirlwind Homes Ltd., Whistler, BC, Canada; PHOTO: © The Taunton Press, Inc.; #2 DESIGN: The Kennebec Company, Bath, ME; PHOTO: Stephen Fazio; #3 DESIGN: Dail Dixon, FAIA, Dixon Weinstein Architects, Chapel Hill, NC; CABINETRY: Aventine Cabinetry, Carrboro, NC; PHOTO: Markatos Photography; #4 DESIGN: Carlene Anderson Kitchen Design, Oakland, CA, and Richard Bartlett, Architect, Orinda, CA; PHOTO: Andrew McKinney

pp. 36-37 #1 DESIGN: Michaela Mahady, Mulfinger, Susanka, Mahady and Partners, Stillwater, MN; PHOTO: © The Taunton Press, Inc.

pp. 38-39 #1 DESIGN: Dail Dixon, FAIA, Dixon Weinstein Associates, Chapel Hill, NC; PHOTO: Markatos Photography; #2 DESIGN: Sloane M. Chambers, Manchester, ME; PHOTO: © The Taunton Press, Inc.; #3 DESIGN: John Seibert, Birdseye Building Company, Richmond, VT; PHOTO: © The Taunton Press, Inc.; #4 DESIGN: Frederic Schwartz, New York, NY; PHOTO: Regina Schrambling; #5 DESIGN: Dail Dixon, FAIA, Dixon Weinstein Associates, Chapel Hill, NC; PHOTO: Markatos Photography

pp. 40-41 #1 DESIGN: Sharon Tyler Hoover, Fayetteville, AR; PHOTO: © The Taunton Press, Inc.; #2 DESIGN: Jeff Morse, Morse and Cleaver, Petaluma, CA; PHOTO: © The Taunton Press, Inc.; #3 DESIGN: Eric Gazley, Gazley Plowman Atkinson, Portland, OR; PHOTO: © The Taunton Press, Inc.; #4 DESIGN: Dail Dixon, FAIA, Dixon Weinstein Assoc., Chapel Hill, NC; PHOTO: Markatos Photography

pp. 42-43 #1 DESIGN: Louis Mackall, Breakfast Woodworks, Guilford, CT; PHOTO: © The Taunton Press, Inc.; #2 DESIGN: Beth Pachacki, Palm Desert, CA; PHOTO: David Duncan Livingston; #3 DESIGN: Peter Twombly, Estes & Company Architects, Newport, RI; PHOTOS: © The Taunton Press, Inc.

pp. 44-45 #1 DESIGN: Ross Chapin, Whidbey Island, WA; PHOTO: © The Taunton Press, Inc.; #2 DESIGN AND PHOTO: John Ferro Sims, London, England; CABINET DESIGN: Egbert Sullivan, Big Egg Designs, London; #3 DESIGN: James Estes, Newport, RI; PHOTO: © The Taunton Press, Inc.; #4 DESIGN: McKee Patterson, AIA, Austin Patterson Disston Architects, Southport, CT; PHOTO: Lizzie Himmel

pp. 46-47 #1 DESIGN: Robert Orr, Robert Orr and Associates, New Haven, CT; PHOTO: © The Taunton Press, Inc.; #2 DESIGN: Defne Veral, A. Defne Veral Interiors, New Haven, CT; CABINETRY: Stephen Peacock, Greenwich, CT; PHOTO: Durston Saylor; #3 DESIGN: Norma DeCamp Burns, FAIA, Raleigh, NC; PHOTOS: Allen Weiss

pp. 48-49 #1 DESIGN: Fu-Tung Cheng and Frank Lee, Cheng Design, Berkeley, CA; PHOTO: © The Taunton Press, Inc.; #2 DESIGN: Thomas Lenchek, Balance Associates, Seattle, WA; PHOTO: © The Taunton Press, Inc.; #3 DESIGN: Stewart Roberts and Karla Johnson, Carlisle, MA; PHOTO: © The Taunton Press, Inc.; #4 DESIGN: Robert W. Knight, Blue Hill, ME; PHOTO: © The Taunton Press, Inc.

pp. 50-51 #1 DESIGN: Judith Landau, Timbercraft Homes, Port Townsend, WA; PHOTO: © The Taunton Press, Inc.; #2 DESIGN: Robert Orr, New Haven, CT; PHOTO: © The Taunton Press, Inc.; #3 DESIGN: Ross Chapin, Whidbey Island, WA; PHOTO: © The Taunton Press, Inc.; #4 DESIGN: Martha B. Finney and Garrett Finney, Philadelphia, PA; PHOTO: © The Taunton Press, Inc.

pp. 52-53 #1 DESIGN: Jeremiah Eck with Paul McNeely, Boston, MA; PHOTO: © The Taunton Press, Inc.; #2 DESIGN: John and Nancy Carney, Carney Architects, Jackson, WY; PHOTO: © The Taunton Press, Inc.; #3 DESIGN: Les Wallach, Line & Space, Tucson, AZ; PHOTOS: Glen Christiansen; #4 DESIGN: Peter Pfeiffer, Barley & Pfeiffer Architects, Austin, TX; PHOTO: © The Taunton Press, Inc.

CABINETS

pp. 54-55 DESIGN: John Seibert, Birdseye Building Co., Richmond, VT; PHOTO: © The Taunton Press, Inc.

pp. 56-57 #1 DESIGN: Dee Singer, The New Kitchen, Greenwich, CT; CABINETRY: Snaidero Cabinets, Italy; PHOTO: Adrianne dePolo; #2 DESIGN: Louis Mackall, Breakfast Woodworks, Guilford, CT; PHOTO: © The Taunton Press, Inc.; #3 DESIGN AND PHOTO: John Ferro Sims, London, England; CABINET DESIGN: Egbert Sullivan, Big Egg Designs, London

pp. 58-59 #1 DESIGN: Joy D. Swallow; Kansas City, MO; CABINETRY: Clarence Swallow, Manhattan, KS; PHOTO: © The Taunton Press, Inc.; #2 DESIGN: Judy Collins, Get A Grip Fine Hardware, Lakewood, CO; PHOTO: courtesy Parrish & Co.; #3 DESIGN: Lou Ann Bauer, ASID, Bauer Interior Design, San Francisco, CA; PHOTO: David Duncan Livingston; #4 DESIGN: The

Kennebec Company, Bath, ME; PHOTO: Stephen Fazio; #5 PHOTO: courtesy Plain & Fancy Custom Cabinetry

pp. 60-61 #1 DESIGN: Bentel & Bentel Architects/ Planners, AIA, Locust Valley, NY; CABINETRY: DAMCA, College Point, NY; PHOTO: Eduard Hueber; #2 DESIGN: David Hall, Henry Klein Partnership, Mt. Vernon, WA; PHOTO: © The Taunton Press, Inc.; #3 DESIGN: Sloane M. Chambers, Manchester, ME; PHOTO: © The Taunton Press, Inc.r; #4 DESIGN: Duo Dickinson, Madison, CT; PHOTO: © The Taunton Press, Inc.; #5 DESIGN AND CABINETRY: John Leontiou, Form Ltd., Greenwich, CT; PHOTO: Brian Urso

pp. 62-63 #1 DESIGN: McKee Patterson, AIA, Austin Patterson Disston Architects, Southport, CT; CABINETRY: James Schriber, New Milford, CT; PHOTO: Lizzie Himmel; #2 DESIGN: Joseph Stevens, Carmel, CA; CABINETRY: Ambrose Pollack, Big Sur, CA; PHOTO: © The Taunton Press, Inc.; #3 DESIGN AND PHOTO: YesterTec Design Company, Center Valley, PA; #4 DESIGN: Edwin Lundie, Minnesota; PHOTO: © The Taunton Press, Inc.; #5 DESIGN: Joni Zimmerman, Design Solutions, Annapolis, MD; TILES: Jackie Smith, Gooseneck Designs, Westminster, MD; CABINETS: Haworth; PHOTO: Bill Schilling

pp. 64-65 #1 DESIGN: Richard Lear, Richard Lear Designs, Southampton, NY; CABINETRY: Peter Craz, Craz Woodworking, Holbrook, NY; PHOTO: Roger Tully; #2 DESIGN AND CABINETRY: Paul Levine; PHOTO: © The Taunton Press, Inc.; #3 DESIGN: Martha B. Finney and Garrett Finney, Philadelphia, PA; PHOTO: © The Taunton Press, Inc.; #5 DESIGNER: William E. Roesner, Newton Centre, MA; CABINETRY: Nathan Rome, Emily Street Woodworkers Cooperative, Cambridge, MA; PHOTO: © The Taunton Press, Inc.; #6 DESIGN: Peter Twombly, Estes & Company Architects, Newport, RI; CABINETRY: Kevin McCullough; PHOTO: © The Taunton Press, Inc.; #7 DESIGN: Robert Knight, Blue Hill, ME; PHOTO: © The Taunton Press, Inc.

pp. 66-67 #1 DESIGN: Ross Chapin, Whidbey Island, WA; PHOTO: © The Taunton Press, Inc.; #2 DESIGN AND CABINETRY: Phillip S. Sollman, Bellefonte, PA; PHOTO: © The Taunton Press, Inc.; #3 DESIGN: Thomas Hughes, Tolovana Park, OR; PHOTO: © The Taunton Press, Inc.

pp. 68-69 #1 DESIGNER: Ross Chapin, Whidbey Island, WA; PHOTO: © The Taunton Press, Inc.; #2 CABINETRY (TOP): Glenbriar, Doylestown, PA (BOTTOM): Superior Woodcraft, Doylestown, PA; #3 DESIGN: Ron Berger, Shutesbury, MA; CABINETRY: Nat Waring; PHOTO: © The Taunton Press, Inc.; #4 DESIGN: Lou Ann Bauer, ASID, Bauer Interior Design, San Francisco, CA; CABINETRY: Nick Yiangou, Mill Valley, CA; FINISH: Baumar Finishing, San Francisco, CA; PHOTO: Jon Jensen; #5 DESIGN: John and Nancy Carney, Carney Architects, Jackson, WY; PHOTO: © The Taunton Press, Inc.

pp. 70-71 #1 DESIGN AND PHOTO: Rob Thallon, Thallon Architects, Eugene, OR; #2 DESIGN AND CABINETRY: Craig W. Murray, Cedar Crest, NM; PULL: Tom Joyce Architectural Blacksmithing, Santa Fe, NM; PHOTO: © The Taunton Press, Inc.; #3 DESIGN: John Johnstone and Lynn Bronfman, Today's Kitchens, Stamford, CT; CABINETRY: Superior Woodcraft, Doylestown, PA; PHOTO: Carolyn Taylor; #4 DESIGN: Brian Brand, Baylis Brand Wagner Architects, Bellevue, WA; PHOTO: © The Taunton Press, Inc.; #5 DESIGN: Bentel & Bentel Architects/ Planners, AIA, Locust Valley, NY; CABINETRY: DAMCA, College Point, NY; PHOTO: Eduard Hueber

pp. 72-73 #1 DESIGN: Kaehler/Moore Architects, Greenwich, CT; CABINETRY: Ram Woodworks, Stratford, CT; PHOTO: Kurt A. Dolnier; #2 DESIGN: Lou Ann Bauer, ASID, Bauer Interior Design, San Francisco, CA; PHOTO: David Duncan Livingston;

#4 DESIGN: Patricia Swalander, Calgary, Alberta, Canada; PHOTO: David Duncan Livingston; #5 DESIGN: John Johnstone and Lynn Bronfman, Today's Kitchens, Stamford, CT; CABINETRY: Superior Woodcraft, Doylestown, PA; #6 DESIGN: Fu-Tung Cheng and Frank Lee, Cheng Design, Berkeley, CA; CABINETRY: Guba/Craig Woodworks, Emeryville, CA; PHOTO: © The Taunton Press, Inc.

pp. 74-75 #1 DESIGN: Fu-Tung Cheng, Cheng Design and Construction, Berkeley, CA; CABINETRY: William Guba and Ross Craig, Oakland, CA; PHOTO: Alan Weintraub; #2 DESIGN: Mark Nettesheim, Carmel, CA; PHOTO: David Duncan Livingston; #3 DESIGN: Lou Ann Bauer, ASID, Bauer Interior Design, San Francisco, CA; CABINETRY: C&M Woodworking, San Francisco, CA; PULLS: Bauerware, San Francisco, CA; PHOTO: Andrew McKinney; #5 DESIGN: John Johnstone & Lynn Bronfman, Today's Kitchens, Stamford, CT; CABINETRY: Superior Woodcraft, Doylestown, PA; PULLS: LB Brass; PHOTO: Carolyn Taylor

pp. 76-77 #1 DESIGN AND CABINETRY: Paul D. Voelker, Chewelah, WA; PHOTO: © The Taunton Press, Inc.; #2 DESIGN: Tamia Marg, San Francisco, CA; PHOTO: © The Taunton Press, Inc.; #3 DESIGN: Judy Collins, Get A Grip Fine Hardware, Lakewood, CO; PHOTO: courtesy Parrish & Co.; #4 DESIGN: Paul Weiner, Tucson, AZ; PHOTO: © The Taunton Press, Inc.; #6 DESIGN AND CONSTRUCTION: Halperin and Christ, San Rafael, CA; PHOTO: Eliot Holtzman; #7 DESIGN: Laurel Quint, Q Design, Denver, CO; CABINET PULLS: Michael Aram for Lewis Dolin, New York, NY; PHOTO: Ellen Jaskol

pp. 78-79 #1 DESIGN: Ernie Rose, Bon Air, VA; PHOTO: © The Taunton Press, Inc.; #2 DESIGN: Bentel & Bentel Architects/Planners, AIA, Locust Valley NY; CABINETRY: DAMCA, College Point, NY; PHOTO: Eduard Hueber; #3 DESIGN: Raymond Beeler and Joanne Douvas, New York, NY; PHOTO: © The Taunton Press, Inc ; #4 DESIGN: Dan Costa, Boston, MA; PHOTO: © The Taunton Press, Inc.

pp. 80-81 #1 DESIGN: Sarah Susanka, Mulfinger, Susanka, Mahady & Partners, Minneapolis, MN; PHOTO: © The Taunton Press, Inc.; #2 DESIGN: Cecilia Campa, Becker/Zeyco Kitchens, San Francisco, CA, PHOTO: David Duncan Livingston; #3 DESIGN: Fran Halperin, Halperin and Christ/Build Design, San Rafael, CA; PHOTO: Mark Becker; #4 DESIGN: Robert Orr & Associates, New Haven, CT; FRIEZE: Lisa Hess, Stony Creek, CT; PHOTO: © The Taunton Press, Inc.; #5 DESIGN: John Leontiou, Form, Ltd., Greenwich, CT; CABINETS: Craftmaid; FAUX PAINTING: Martha Fohn; PHOTO: Brian Urso

pp. 82-83 #1 DESIGN: Kaehler/Moore Architects, Greenwich, CT; CABINETRY: Ram Woodworks, Stratford, CT; PHOTO: Kurt A. Dolnier; #2 DESIGN: Richard Lear, Richard Lear Designs, Southampton, NY; CABINETRY: Peter Craz, Craz Woodworking, Holbrook, NY; PHOTO: Roger Tully; #3 DESIGN: Fred Thornton Hollingsworth, North Vancouver, BC, Canada; PHOTO: © The Taunton Press, Inc.; #4 DESIGN: James Estes, Newport, RI; PHOTO: © The Taunton Press, Inc.

pp. 84-85 #1 DESIGN: Peter Cardamone and Cynthia Curley, Bluebell Kitchens, Springhouse, PA; PHOTO: Baruch Schwartz; #2 DESIGN: Judith Landau, Timbercraft Homes, Port Townsend, WA; PHOTO: © The Taunton Press, Inc.; #3 DESIGN: Derek Van Alstine, Santa Cruz, CA; PHOTO: © The Taunton Press, Inc.; #4 DESIGN: Jonathan Livingston, San Francisco, CA; PHOTO: © The Taunton Press, Inc.; #5 DESIGN: McKee Patterson, AIA, Austin Patterson Disston Architects, Southport, CT; CABINETRY: Owen Gardella, Manitou Construction, Roxbury, CT; PHOTO: John Kane

pp. 86-87 #1 DESIGN: Cecilia Campa, Becker/Zeyco Kitchens, San Francisco, CA; PHOTO: David Duncan Livingston; #2 DESIGN: Victor Demasi, West Redding, CT; PHOTO: © The Taunton Press, Inc.; #3 CABINETRY: Merrillat, Adrian, MI; #4 DESIGN: Michael P. Johnson, Cave Creek, AZ; PHOTO: © The Taunton Press, Inc.

pp. 88-89 #1, #2 DESIGN AND CABINETRY: The Kennebec Company, Bath, ME; PHOTO: Stephen Fazio; #3 DESIGN: Jerri Holan, Albany, CA; PHOTO: © The Taunton Press, Inc.; #4 DESIGN: Sharon Tyler Hoover, Fayetteville, AR; PHOTO: © The Taunton Press, Inc.

pp. 90-91 #1 DESIGN: Lou Ann Bauer, ASID, Bauer Interior Design, San Francisco, CA; CABINETRY: Nick Yiangou, Mill Valley, CA; PHOTO: Jon Jensen; #2 DESIGN AND PHOTO: Haworth Country Furniture, Margate, FL; #3 DESIGN: John Johnstone & Lynn Bronfman, Today's Kitchens, Stamford, CT; CABINETRY: Superior Woodcraft, Doylestown, PA; PHOTO: Larry Frankel; #4 PHOTO: courtesy Norcraft Companies, Inc.

pp. 92-93 #1 DESIGN AND CABINETRY: The Kennebec Company, Bath, ME; PHOTO: Stephen Fazio; #2 DESIGN: Allan Greenberg, Architect (David Harlan, project architect), Greenwich, CT; CONSTRUCTION: Robert Weinstein, Truro, MA; PHOTO: © The Taunton Press, Inc.; #3 DESIGN: Kaehler/Moore Architects, Greenwich, CT; METALWORKING: John Orphanu, Promet, Milford, CT; CABINET CASES: St. Charles; PHOTO: Durston Saylor; #4 DESIGNER: Bentel & Bentel Architects/Planners, AIA, Locust Valley NY; CABINETRY: Shoichi Hamano, Oh-Show Woodworking, New York, NY; PHOTO: Eduard Hueber; #5 DESIGN AND CABINETRY: John Leontiou, Form Ltd., Greenwich, CT; PHOTO: Brian Urso

pp. 94-95 #1 DESIGN AND CABINETRY: Sam Clark; PHOTO: © The Taunton Press, Inc.; #2 PHOTOS (TOP AND MIDDLE): courtesy Plain & Fancy Custom Cabinetry; DESIGN (BOTTOM): Joy D. Swallow, Kansas City, MO; PHOTO: © The Taunton Press, Inc.; #3 DESIGN: Tobin T. Dougherty, Palo Alto, CA; PHOTOS: © The Taunton Press, Inc.

pp. 96-97 #1 DESIGN: Fu-Tung Cheng and Frank Lee, Cheng Design, Berkeley, CA; CABINETRY: Guba/Craig Woodworks, Emeryville, CA; PHOTOS: © The Taunton Press, Inc.; #2 PHOTO (LEFT): courtesy Plain & Fancy Custom Cabinetry; DESIGN (RIGHT): Daryl Ann Letts, Showcase Kitchens, Climax, MI; PHOTO: David Duncan Livingston; #3 DESIGN: Janet Moody, Menlo Park, CA; PHOTOS: © The Taunton Press, Inc.; #4 PHOTO: courtesy Norcraft Companies, Inc.

pp. 98-99 #1 DESIGN: William E. Roesner, Newton Centre, MA; CABINETRY: Nathan Rome, Emily Street Woodworkers Cooperative, Cambridge, MA; PHOTO: © The Taunton Press, Inc.; #2 DESIGN: Neal Metal, Ltd., San Francisco, CA; PHOTO: David Duncan Livingston; #3 PHOTO: courtesy Norcraft Companies, Inc.; #4 DESIGN: Neal Metal, Ltd., San Francisco, CA; PHOTO: David Duncan Livingston; #5 DESIGN AND CABINETRY: Paul D. Voelker; Chewelah, WA; Voelker, PHOTO: © The Taunton Press, Inc.

SHELVES AND PANTRIES

pp. 100-101 DESIGN: John & Nancy Carney, Carney Architects, Jackson, WY; PHOTO: © The Taunton Press, Inc.

pp. 102-103 #1 DESIGN: Rolf Kielman, Truex Cullins & Partners Architects, Burlington, VT; PHOTO: Becky Luigart-Stayner; #2 DESIGN AND CONSTRUCTION: South Mountain Company, Chilmark, MA; PHOTO: Jennifer Levy; #3 DESIGN AND CONSTRUC-

TION: South Mountain Company, Chilmark, MA; **PHOTO:** Derrill Bazzy

pp. 104-105 #1 DESIGN: Victoria Holland, Bellevue, WA; **PHOTO:** © The Taunton Press, Inc.; **#2 DESIGN:** Dail Dixon, FAIA, Dixon Weinstein Associates, Chapel Hill, NC; **PHOTO:** Markatos Photography; **#3 DESIGN:** Sloane M. Chambers, Manchester, ME; **PHOTO:** © The Taunton Press, Inc.; **#4 DESIGN:** Jonathan Livingston, San Francisco, CA; **PHOTO:** © The Taunton Press, Inc.; **#5 DESIGN:** Rolf Kielman, Truex Cullins & Partners Architects, Burlington, VT; **PHOTO:** Becky Luigart-Stayner; **#6 DESIGN AND CABINETRY:** John Leontiou, Form Ltd., Greenwich, CT; **PHOTO:** Brian Urso

pp. 106-107 #1 DESIGN: Tim Joseph and Rex Alexander, Brethren, MI; **PHOTO:** Tom Kachadurian; **#2 DESIGN AND CONSTRUCTION:** South Mountain Company, Chilmark, MA; **PHOTO:** Derrill Bazzy **#4 DESIGN:** Brad Sills, Whirlwind Homes Ltd., Whistler, BC, Canada; **PHOTO:** © The Taunton Press, Inc.

pp. 108-109 #1 DESIGN: David Hall, Henry Klein Partnership, Mount Vernon, WA; **PHOTO:** © The Taunton Press, Inc.; **#2 DESIGN:** F. John Richards (Architect), Portola Valley, CA; Fu-Tung Cheng, Cheng Design & Construction, Inc., Berkeley, CA; **STEEL SHELVES:** B&S Metals; **PHOTO:** Alan Weintraub; **#3 DESIGN:** Michael P. Johnson, Cave Creek, AZ; **PHOTO:** © The Taunton Press, Inc.; **#4 DESIGN:** William E. Roesner, Newton Centre, MA; **PHOTO:** © The Taunton Press, Inc.; **#5 DESIGN:** Ron Berger, Shutesbury, MA; **PHOTO:** © The Taunton Press, Inc.; **#7 DESIGN:** Arnelle Kase, Barbara Scavullo Design, San Francisco, CA; **PHOTO:** David Duncan Livingston; **#8 DESIGN:** Richard and Elizabeth O'Leary, Croton Falls, NY; **PHOTO:** Richard O'Leary

pp. 110-111 #1 DESIGN AND CONSTRUCTION: South Mountain Co., Chilmark, MA; **PHOTO:** Derrill Bazzy; **#2 DESIGN:** Charles Aquino, Richmond, VA; **PHOTO:** © The Taunton Press, Inc.; **#3 DESIGN:** Robert Orr, Robert Orr & Associates, New Haven, CT; **PAINTED FRIEZE:** Lisa Hess, Stony Creek, CT; **PHOTO:** © The Taunton Press, Inc.

pp. 112-113 #2 DESIGN: Sarah Reep, Starmark, Inc., Northwood, IA; **PHOTO:** David Duncan Livingston; **#3 DESIGN:** Candra Scott, San Francisco, CA; **CABINETRY:** Jim Sellars, San Francisco, CA; **PHOTO:** David Duncan Livingston; **#4 DESIGN AND CONSTRUCTION:** South Mountain Company, Chilmark, MA; **PHOTO:** Ray Kellman; **#5 PHOTO:** courtesy Norcraft Companies, Inc.

pp. 114-115 #1 DESIGN: John and Nancy Carney, Carney Architects, Jackson, WY; **PHOTO:** © The Taunton Press, Inc.; **#2 DESIGN:** Kaehler/Moore Architects, Greenwich, CT; **CABINETRY:** Coastal Woodworks, Bridgeport, CT; **PULL-OUT PANTRY HARDWARE:** Häfele; **PHOTO:** Durston Saylor; **#3 DESIGN:** William E. Roesner, Newton Centre, MA; **CABINETRY:** Nathan Rome, Emily Street Woodworkers Cooperative, Cambridge, MA; **PHOTO:** © The Taunton Press, Inc.

COUNTERTOPS AND BACKSPLASHES

pp. 116-117 DESIGN: Fu-Tung Cheng with Janet Szalay and Chris Tong, Cheng Design, Berkeley, CA; **STAINLESS-STEEL COUNTERTOP:** Andrus Sheet Metal, Richmond, CA; **CONCRETE COUNTERTOP:** Cheng Design & Construction; **PHOTO:** J. D. Peterson.

pp. 118-119 #1 DESIGN: Rob Thallon, Eugene, OR; **STAINLESS STEEL:** Foy Martin Sheet Metal, Springfield, OR; **PHOTO:** © The Taunton Press, Inc.; **#2 DESIGN:** Louis Mackall, Breakfast Woodworks, Guilford, CT; **PHOTO:** © The Taunton Press, Inc.; **#3 DESIGN:** Lou Ann Bauer, ASID, Bauer Interior

Design, San Francisco, CA; **TILE:** American Slate, San Francisco, CA; **INSTALLATION:** Peter Whitehead, San Francisco, CA; **PHOTO:** Andrew McKinney; **#4 DESIGN:** Lou Ann Bauer, ASID, Bauer Interior Design, San Francisco, CA; **PHOTO:** Andrew McKinney

pp. 120-121 #1 DESIGN: Victoria Holland, Bellevue, WA; **PHOTO:** © The Taunton Press, Inc.; **#3 DESIGN:** Eric Gazley, Gazley Plowman Atkinson, Portland, OR; **PHOTO:** © The Taunton Press, Inc.; **#4 DESIGN:** McKee Patterson, AIA, Austin Patterson Disston Architects, Southport, CT; **PHOTO:** Lizzie Himmel

pp. 122-123 #1 DESIGN: Ross Chapin, Whidbey Island, WA; **PHOTO:** © The Taunton Press, Inc.; **#2 DESIGN:** Robert W. Knight, Blue Hill, ME; **PHOTO:** © The Taunton Press, Inc.; **#3 DESIGN:** Sarah Susanka, Mulfinger, Susanka, Mahady & Partners, Minneapolis, MN; **PHOTO:** © The Taunton Press, Inc.

pp. 124-125 #1 DESIGN: Max Jacobson and Doug Shaffer, Jacobson, Silverstein, Winslow Architects, Berkeley, CA; **PHOTO:** © The Taunton Press, Inc.; **#2 DESIGN:** Sarah Reep, Starmark, Inc., Northwood, IA; **PHOTO:** David Duncan Livingston; **#4 DESIGN:** Looney Ricks Kiss Architects, Memphis, TN; **PHOTO:** Jeffrey Jacobs/Architectural Photography; **#5 PHOTO:** courtesy Wilsonart International; **#6 DESIGN:** Sam Clark, Plainville, VT; **PHOTO:** © The Taunton Press, Inc.

pp. 126-127 #1 DESIGN: Peter Cardamone and Cynthia Curley, Bluebell Kitchens, Springhouse, PA; **PHOTO:** Baruch Schwartz; **#2 DESIGN:** Michael P. Johnson, Cave Creek, AZ; **PHOTO:** © The Taunton Press, Inc.; **#3 DESIGN:** Joseph Greene, Lopez Island, WA; **PHOTO:** © The Taunton Press, Inc.; **#4 DESIGN:** Fu-Tung Cheng and Frank Lee, Cheng Design, Berkeley, CA; **CABINETRY:** Guba/Craig Woodworks, Emeryville, CA; **PHOTO:** © The Taunton Press, Inc.

pp. 128-129 #1 DESIGN: Fu-Tung Cheng with Janet Szalay and Chris Tong, Cheng Design, Berkeley, CA; **PHOTO:** J. D. Peterson; **#3 DESIGN:** Cecilia Campa, Becker/Zeyco Kitchens; **PHOTO:** David Duncan Livingston; **#4 DESIGN:** Fu-Tung Cheng with Janet Szalay and Chris Tong, Cheng Design, Berkeley, CA; **CONCRETE COUNTERTOP:** Cheng Design & Construction; **STAINLESS-STEEL SINK AND COUNTERS:** Andrus Sheet Metal, Richmond, CA; **PHOTO:** J. D. Peterson

pp. 130-131 #1 DESIGN: Peter Cardamone and Cynthia Curley, Bluebell Kitchens, Springhouse, PA; **PHOTO:** Baruch Schwartz; **#2 TILES:** Jackie Smith, Gooseneck Designs, Westminster, MD; **KITCHEN DESIGN:** Joni Zimmerman, Design Solutions, Annapolis, MD; **PHOTO:** Bill Schilling; **#3 DESIGN:** Tom Meehan, Westport Tile & Design, Westport, CT; **TILES:** imported by Country Floors, New York, NY; **PHOTO:** © The Taunton Press, Inc.; **#4 DESIGN:** Lou Ann Bauer, ASID, Bauer Interior Design, San Francisco, CA; **PHOTO:** David Duncan Livingston; **#5 DESIGN:** Art for Living/Julie Atwood Design, Glen Ellen, CA; **PHOTO:** David Duncan Livingston

pp. 132-133 #1 DESIGN: A. Defne Veral Interiors, New Haven, CT; **PHOTO:** Durston Saylor; **#2 DESIGN:** Robert Orr & Associates, New Haven, CT; **TILES:** Fulper Glazes, Yardley, PA; **PHOTO:** © The Taunton Press, Inc.; **#3 DESIGN:** Eric Gazley, Gazley Plowman Atkinson, Portland, OR; **PHOTO:** © The Taunton Press, Inc.; **#4 TILES:** Melinda Ashley, Waltham, MA; **PHOTO:** Roe A. Osborn; **#5 TILES:** Melinda Ashley, Waltham, MA; **PHOTO:** © The Taunton Press, Inc.; **#6 DESIGN AND CONSTRUCTION:** South Mountain Company, Chilmark, MA; **PHOTO:** Derrill Bazzy

pp. 134-135 #1 DESIGN: Peter Cardamone and Cynthia Curley, Bluebell Kitchens, Springhouse, PA; **PHOTO:** Baruch Schwartz; **#2 DESIGN:** Brian Brand, Baylis Brand Wagner Architects, Bellevue, WA; **PHOTO:** © The Taunton Press, Inc.; **#3 DESIGN:** Kurt Lavenson and Cass Smith, Alamo, CA; **PHOTO:** © The Taunton

Press, Inc.; **#4 DESIGN AND CONSTRUCTION:** South Mountain Company, Chilmark, MA; **PHOTO:** Derrill Bazzy; **#5 DESIGN:** John Johnstone & Lynn Bronfman, Today's Kitchens, Stamford, CT; **PHOTO:** Larry Frankel

pp. 136-137 #1 DESIGN: Sharon Tyler Hoover, Fayetteville, AR; **PHOTO:** © The Taunton Press, Inc.; **#2 DESIGN:** F. John Richards (Architect), Portola Valley, CA; Fu-Tung Cheng, Cheng Design & Construction, Inc., Berkeley, CA; **PHOTO:** Alan Weintraub; **#4 PHOTO:** David Duncan Livingston; **#5 DESIGN:** John Seibert, Birdseye Building Company, Richmond, VT; **PHOTO:** © The Taunton Press, Inc.

pp. 138-139 #1 DESIGN AND COUNTERTOP CONSTRUCTION: Rob Thallon, Eugene, OR; **PHOTOS:** © The Taunton Press, Inc.; **#2 DESIGN:** Sloane M. Chambers, Manchester, ME; **PHOTO:** © The Taunton Press, Inc.; **#3 DESIGN:** Thomas Hughes, Tolovana Park, OR; **PHOTO:** © The Taunton Press, Inc.; **#4 COUNTERTOP AND BACKSPLASH:** Buddy Rhodes; **PHOTO:** Apollo Icdag; **#5 DESIGN:** Bruce Goodwin, New Orleans, LA; **PHOTO:** Tim Mueller

pp. 140-141 #1 DESIGN: Fu-Tung Cheng and Frank Lee, Cheng Design, Berkeley, CA; **COUNTERTOP:** Cheng Design and Construction; **PHOTO:** © The Taunton Press, Inc.; **#2 DESIGN:** Crescent Rock, Chicago; **PHOTO:** Leto/Craig, Chicago (courtesy Soupcan, Inc.); **#3 DESIGN:** Buddy Rhodes Studio, San Francisco, CA; **TILE:** Classico Tile, Columbus, OH; **PHOTO:** Rod Joslin; **#4 DESIGN:** Phillip S. Sollman, Bellefonte, PA; **PHOTO:** © The Taunton Press, Inc.; **#5 DESIGN:** Crescent Rock, Chicago; **PHOTO:** Leto/Craig, Chicago (courtesy Soupcan, Inc.)

APPLIANCES AND SINKS

pp. 142-143 DESIGN: Paul Bierman-Lytle, New Canaan, CT; **PHOTO:** © The Taunton Press, Inc.

pp. 144-145 #1 DESIGN: Ernie Rose, Bon Air, VA; **PHOTO:** © The Taunton Press, Inc.; **#2 DESIGN:** Rex Alexander, Brethren, MI; **PHOTO:** © The Taunton Press, Inc.; **#3 DESIGN:** John Johnstone and Lynn Bronfman, Today's Kitchens, Stamford, CT; **CABINETRY:** Superior Woodcraft; **PHOTO:** Carolyn Taylor

pp. 146-147 #1 DESIGN: Fu-Tung Cheng and Frank Lee, Cheng Design, Berkeley, CA; **CABINETRY:** Guba/Craig Woodworks, Emeryville, CA; **PHOTO:** © The Taunton Press, Inc.; **#2 DESIGN:** Phillip S. Sollman, Bellefonte, PA; **PHOTO:** © The Taunton Press, Inc.; **#3 DESIGN:** Robert Orr & Associates, New Haven CT; **PHOTO:** © The Taunton Press, Inc.; **#4 DESIGN:** Art for Living/Julie Atwood Design, Glen Ellen, CA; **PHOTO:** David Duncan Livingston; **#5 DESIGN:** Camperti Associates, San Rafael, CA; **PHOTO:** David Duncan Livingston

pp. 148-149 #1 DESIGN: McKee Patterson, AIA, Austin Patterson Disston Architects, Southport, CT; **PHOTO:** Lizzie Himmel; **#2 DESIGN:** The Kennebec Company; Bath, ME; **PHOTO:** Stephen Fazio; **#3 PHOTO:** courtesy EuropeanLiving Limited, Oldwick, NJ

pp. 150-151 #1 DESIGN: Joseph Stevens, Carmel, CA; **CABINETRY:** Ambrose Pollack, Big Sur, CA; **PHOTO:** © The Taunton Press, Inc.; **#2 PHOTO:** courtesy Kohler, Co.; **#4 FAUCET:** Czech and Speake, Waterworks; **PHOTO:** Joanne Kellar Bouknight; **#5 DESIGN:** Rob Wilkinson, Wilkinson & Hartman, San Rafael, CA; **PHOTO:** David Duncan Livingston; **#6 PHOTO:** courtesy Rapetti Faucet, George Blotcher, Inc., Plainville, MA

pp. 152-153 #1 DESIGN: Robert Orr & Associates, New Haven, CT; **PHOTO:** © The Taunton Press, Inc.; **#2 DESIGN:** Roger Whipple; **PHOTO:**

© The Taunton Press, Inc.; **#3** DESIGN: Sloane M. Chambers, Manchester, ME; PHOTO: © The Taunton Press, Inc.; **#4** DESIGN: Phillip S. Sollman, Bellefonte, PA; PHOTO: © The Taunton Press, Inc.

pp. 154-155 **#1** DESIGN: Douglas Small, Kennett Square, PA; PHOTO: © The Taunton Press, Inc.; **#2** DESIGN: Paul Weiner, Tucson, AZ; PHOTO: © The Taunton Press, Inc.; **#3** DESIGN: Peter Cardamone, Bluebell Kitchens, Springhouse, PA, and Michael Hauptman, Brawer and Hauptman, Philadelphia, PA; PHOTO: Barry Halkin; **#5** DESIGN: Fu-Tung Cheng with Frank Lee, Cheng Design, Berkeley, CA; PHOTO: © The Taunton Press, Inc.

pp. 156-157 **#1** DESIGN: Peter Cardamone, Bluebell Kitchens, Springhouse, PA, and Michael Hauptman, Brawer and Hauptman, Philadelphia, PA; PHOTO: Barry Halkin; **#2** DESIGN AND CONSTRUCTION: South Mountain Company, Chilmark, MA; PHOTO: Randi Baird; **#3** DESIGN: Mark Nettesheim, Carmel, CA; PHOTO: David Duncan Livingston; **#4** DESIGN: John Douglas, Tucson, AZ; PHOTO: Mark Boisclair; **#5** DESIGN: William E. Roesner, Newton Centre, MA; FAN RESTORATION: William Sweeney, The Yankee Craftsman, Wayland, MA; PHOTO: © The Taunton Press, Inc.

pp. 158-159 **#2** DESIGN: Peter Cardamone, Bluebell Kitchens, Springhouse PA; PHOTO: Baruch Schwartz; **#3** DESIGN: McKee Patterson, AIA, Austin Patterson Disston Architects, Southport, CT; PHOTO: Lizzie Himmel; **#4** DESIGN: Rolf Kielman, Truex Cullins & Partners Architects, Burlington, VT; PHOTO: Becky Luigart-Stayner

pp. 160-161 **#1** DESIGN: Joseph Stevens, Carmel, CA; PHOTO: © The Taunton Press, Inc.; **#2** DESIGN: Peter Cardamone, Bluebell Kitchens, Springhouse, PA; PHOTO: Baruch Schwartz; **#3** DESIGN: McKee Patterson, AIA, Austin Patterson Disston Architects, Southport, CT; PHOTO: Lizzie Himmel; **#5** DESIGN: Rolf Kielman, Truex Cullins & Partners Architects, Burlington, VT; PHOTO: Becky Luigart-Stayner

pp. 162-163 **#1** DESIGN: Camperti Associates, San Rafael, CA; PHOTO: David Duncan Livingston; **#2** DESIGN: Kaehler/Moore Architects, Greenwich, CT; PHOTO: George Dumitru; **#3** DESIGN AND CABINETRY: John Leontiou, Form Ltd., Greenwich, CT; PHOTO: Brian Urso; **#4** DESIGN: Eric Rekdahl, Christopherson and Graff Architects, Berkeley, CA; PHOTO: © The Taunton Press, Inc.r; **#5** DESIGN: William E. Roesner, Newton Centre, MA; PHOTO: © The Taunton Press, Inc.; **#6** DESIGN: Kaehler/Moore Architects, Greenwich, CT; PHOTO: George Dumitru

pp. 164-165 **#1** DESIGN: Joseph Stevens, Carmel, CA; PHOTO: © The Taunton Press, Inc.; **#2** DESIGN: Rob Thallon, Eugene, OR; PHOTO: © The Taunton Press, Inc.; **#3** DESIGN: Sloane M. Chambers, Manchester, ME; PHOTO: © The Taunton Press, Inc.; **#4** DESIGN: Gordon Lagerquist, Lagerquist and Morris, Seattle, WA; PHOTO: © The Taunton Press, Inc.; **#5** DESIGN: Rolf Kielman, Truex Cullins & Partners Architects, Burlington, VT; PHOTO: Becky Luigart-Stayner; **#6** DESIGN: Wharton Esherick, Paoli, PA; PHOTO: © The Taunton Press, Inc.

FLOORS, WALLS, AND CEILINGS

pp. 166-167 DESIGN: Lou Ann Bauer, ASID, Bauer Interior Design, San Francisco, CA; WALL AND CEILING FIXTURES: Artdecor, Berkeley, CA; PHOTO: David Duncan Livingston

pp. 168-169 **#1** DESIGN: Paul Weiner, Design & Building Consultants Inc., Tucson, AZ; PHOTO: © The Taunton Press, Inc.; **#2** DESIGN: Dee Singer,

The New Kitchen, Greenwich, CT; PHOTO: Adrianne dePolo; **#3** DESIGN: Scott Waterman and Brett Landenberger; PHOTO: David Duncan Livingston; **#4** DESIGN: Lou Ann Bauer, ASID, Bauer Interior Design, San Francisco, CA; FLOOR: Baumar Finishing, San Francisco, CA; PHOTO: Andrew McKinney

pp. 170-171 **#1** DESIGN: Laurie Crogan, Los Angeles, CA; PHOTOS: © The Taunton Press, Inc.; **#2** DESIGN: Rolf Kielman, Truex Cullins & Partners Architects, Burlington, VT; PHOTO: Joanne Kellar Bouknight; **#3** DESIGN: Jan Regis, Binns Designer Kitchens, Pickering, ON, Canada; PHOTO: David Duncan Livingston; **#5** PHOTO: courtesy Congoleum Corp.

pp. 172-173 **#1** DESIGN: Lou Ann Bauer, ASID, Bauer Interior Design, San Francisco, CA; FLOOR, CABINET FINISHES: Baumar Finishing, San Francisco, CA; PHOTO: Andrew McKinney; **#2** DESIGN: Susan N. Smith and Ernst A. Benzien, Homeworks Associates, Santa Barbara, CA; PHOTO: © The Taunton Press, Inc.; **#3** DESIGN: Alan Greenberg (David Harlan, project architect), Greenwich, CT; CONSTRUCTION: Robert Weinstein, Roberts Associates Builders, Truro, MD; FLOOR: Jonathan Grumette, BABA Floors, Pittsboro, NC; PHOTO: © The Taunton Press, Inc.; **#4** DESIGN: William Dutcher, Berkeley, CA; PHOTO: © The Taunton Press, Inc.; **#5** DESIGN: Gary Catchpole, Old Greenwich, CT; PAINTED FLOOR: Christine Butcher; PHOTO: Joanne Kellar Bouknight

pp. 174-175 **#1** DESIGN: Joseph Greene, Lopez Island, WA; PHOTO: © The Taunton Press, Inc.; **#2** DESIGN: Catherine Macfee, Macfee and Associates Interior Design, Lafayette, CA; PHOTO: David Duncan Livingston; **#3** DESIGN: William E. Roesner, Newton Centre, MA; PHOTO: © The Taunton Press, Inc.; **#4** DESIGN: Beth Pachacki, Palm Desert, CA; PHOTO: David Duncan Livingston; **#6** DESIGN: Rolf Kielman, Truox Collinc & Partnoro Architects, Burlington, VT; BUILDER: Dan Morris, Roundtree Construction Inc., New Haven, VT; PHOTO: Becky Luigart-Stayner

pp. 176-177 **#1** DESIGN: Fu-Tung Cheng with Janet Szalay and Chris Tong; Cheng Design, Berkeley, CA; CONCRETE FLOOR: Cheng Design & Construction, Berkeley, CA; PHOTO: J. D. Peterson; **#2** DESIGN: Sloane M. Chambers, Manchester, ME; PHOTO: © The Taunton Press, Inc.; **#3** DESIGN: Judith Landau, Timbercraft Homes, Port Townsend, WA; PHOTO: © The Taunton Press, Inc.; **#5** DESIGN AND CONSTRUCTION: Chris Prokosch and Shannon Green, DesignWorks Construction, Floyd, VA; PHOTO: © The Taunton Press, Inc.

pp. 178-179 **#1** DESIGN: Lynn Hopkins, Arlington, MA; PHOTO: © The Taunton Press, Inc.; **#2** DESIGN: McKee Patterson, AIA, Austin Patterson Disston Architects, Southport, CT; PHOTO: John Kane; **#3** DESIGN: Jan Regis, Binns Designer Kitchens and Baths, Pickering, ON, Canada; CONSTRUCTION: Colin Bird, Toronto, ON, Canada; PHOTO: David Duncan Livingston

pp. 180-181 **#1** DESIGN: Fu-Tung Cheng with Frank Lee and Alice Soohoo, Cheng Design, Berkeley, CA; CONCRETE: Gene S. Carranza Construction; PHOTO: Debbie Beachum; **#2** DESIGN: Defne Veral, A. Defne Veral Interiors, New Haven, CT ; PHOTO: Durston Saylor; **#3** DESIGN: Laurel Quint, Q Design, Denver, CO; PHOTO: Ellen Jaskol; **#4** DESIGN: Lou Ann Bauer, ASID, Bauer Interior Design, San Francisco, CA; PHOTO: Andrew McKinney; **#5** DESIGN: Joseph Stevens, Carmel, CA; PHOTO: Charles Miller

LIGHT IN THE KITCHEN

pp. 182-183 DESIGN: Jonathan Livingston, San Francisco, CA; PHOTO: © The Taunton Press, Inc.

pp. 184-185 **#1** DESIGN: Rob Thallon, Eugene, OR; CONSTRUCTION: Kevin McGraw, Eugene, OR; PHOTO: © The Taunton Press, Inc.; **#2** DESIGN AND CONSTRUCTION: Tony Simmonds, Domus, Vancouver, BC, Canada; PHOTOS: © The Taunton Press, Inc.

pp. 186-187 **#1** DESIGN: Alan Greenberg (David Harlan, project architect); Greenwich, CT; CONSTRUCTION: Robert Weinstein, Roberts Associates Builders, Truro, MA; PHOTO: © The Taunton Press, Inc.; **#2** DESIGN: Sloane M. Chambers, Manchester, ME; TRANSLUCENT PANELS: Kalwall, Manchester, NH; PHOTO: © The Taunton Press, Inc.; **#3** DESIGN AND CONSTRUCTION: Alan Jencks, Berkeley, CA; PHOTO: © The Taunton Press, Inc.; **#4** DESIGN AND CONSTRUCTION: South Mountain Company, Chilmark, MA; PHOTO: Dennis Thulin; **#5** DESIGN: William Dutcher, Berkeley, CA; PHOTO: © The Taunton Press, Inc.

pp. 188-189 **#1** DESIGN: Thomas Lenchek, Balance Associates, Seattle, WA; PHOTO: © The Taunton Press, Inc.; **#2** DESIGN: David Weiser, West Vancouver, BC, Canada; PHOTO: © The Taunton Press, Inc.; **#3** DESIGN: Dee Singer, The New Kitchen, Greenwich, CT; PHOTO: Adrianne dePolo; **#5** DESIGN: Jeff Gold, Nevada City, CA; PHOTO: © The Taunton Press, Inc.; **#6** DESIGN: Victoria Holland, Bellevue, WA; PHOTO: © The Taunton Press, Inc.

pp. 190-191 **#1** DESIGN AND CONSTRUCTION: South Mountain Company, Chilmark, MA; PHOTO: Derrill Bazzy; **#2** DESIGN AND CONSTRUCTION: Jonathan Livingston, San Francisco, CA; PHOTO: © The Taunton Press, Inc.; **#3** DESIGN: Eric Gazley, Gazley Plowman Atkinson, Portland, OR; PHOTO: © The Taunton Press, Inc.; **#4** DESIGN: Cecilia Campa, Becker/Zeyco Kitchens, San Francisco, CA; PHOTO: David Duncan Livingston

pp. 192-193 **#1** DESIGN: Lou Ann Bauer, ASID, Bauer Interior Design, San Francisco, CA; LIGHT FIXTURE: Geoffrey Jones, Architrave, San Francisco, CA; PHOTO: Andrew McKinney; **#2** FISH/DESIGN FABRICATION: Scott McDowell, Martha's Vineyard, MA; PHOTO: © The Taunton Press, Inc.; **#3** DESIGN: Joseph Stevens, Carmel, CA; PHOTO: © The Taunton Press, Inc.; **#4** DESIGN: Cheng Design & Construction, Inc., Berkeley, CA; ARCHITECTURE: F. John Richards, Portola Valley, CA; LOW-VOLTAGE LIGHTING: Gage Cauchois Design; HOOD: Cheng Design; PHOTO: Alan Weintraub

pp. 194-195 **#1** DESIGN: Norma DeCamp Burns, FAIA, Raleigh, NC; PHOTO: Allen Weiss; **#3** DESIGN: Laurel Quint, Q Design, Denver, CO; MOSAIC DESIGN: Michael Golden, Michael R. Golden Design, New York, NY; PHOTO: Ellen Jaskol; **#4** DESIGN: John Seibert, Birdseye Building Company, Richmond, VT; PHOTO: © The Taunton Press, Inc.; **#5** DESIGN: Martha B. Finney and Garrett Finney, Philadelphia, PA; PHOTO: © The Taunton Press, Inc.; **#6** DESIGN: Heidi Richardson, Richardson Architects, Sausalito, CA; PHOTO: David Duncan Livingston

PUBLISHER
JIM CHILDS

ACQUISITIONS EDITOR
STEVE CULPEPPER

EDITORIAL ASSISTANT
CAROL KASPER

EDITORS
PETER CHAPMAN, THOMAS McKENNA

DESIGNER/LAYOUT ARTIST
HENRY ROTH

ILLUSTRATOR
JOANNE KELLAR BOUKNIGHT

TYPEFACE
BERLING

PAPER
70-LB. OPUS MATTE

PRINTER
R. R. DONNELLEY, WILLARD, OHIO